Parenting Rules!

The Hilarious
Handbook
for Surviving
Parenthood

RYAN O'QUINN

BroadStreet
PUBLISHING

BroadStreet Publishing Group LLC
Racine, WI 53403
Broadstreetpublishing.com

Parenting Rules!

The Hilarious Handbook for Surviving Parenthood
© 2014 Ryan O'Quinn

ISBN 978-1-4245-4998-6
e-ISBN 978-1-4245-5002-9

Illustrations by Paul Manchester | www.wilwhimsey.com
Design by Chris Garborg | www.garborgdesign.com

Printed in China

FOR
Lilah,
Harry,
AND
Asher

These commandments that I give you today
are to be on your hearts. Impress them on
your children. Talk about them when you sit
at home and when you walk along the road,
when you lie down and when you get up.

Deuteronomy 6:6-7 NIV

When my two oldest children were two years old and six months old, I realized that there are similar and hysterically funny things that all parents go through. These kinds of shared experiences give parents a common bond that is indescribable—except in terms of smell. Step back and actually think about the ridiculous things that happen in your household on a daily basis. To some people, you sound crazy. To other parents, the everyday moments you describe sound absolutely normal.

As I jotted down funny and endearing moments that happened with my kids and posted them on various social networking sites, the comments were all to the tune of "Amen!" and "Me too!" and "That's really gross! Please never post again!" from parents all over the country. It seems that we are all experiencing the same things as we navigate a season in our lives that defies logic, science, and sanity. I thought there was something uniquely nuts about what was happening under my roof, yet I saw I wasn't the only one going through it. All of us brave enough to bear offspring are enrolled in the humbling, absurd school called Parenting University—where grades are given in hugs and kisses on the cheek, in addition to dirty diapers and backhanded compliments.

Once, in the middle of the night, my wife and I were exhausted. We had been out of bed and down the hall to the kids' room too many times to count; swaddling, comforting, and reinserting a pacifier (into the right end, I hoped). There in the hallway, I pulled out my phone and started making notes of what I call "Parenting Rules." If you are a parent, are planning to be a parent, have ever known a parent, or had a parent, the "rules" in these pages were written for you. What started as comical notes for myself became a collection of moments and stories I am now sharing with you in the hope that you will declare, "Ryan, you are not alone. I understand where you're coming from." I hope these rules make you smile or even laugh out loud the next time you find yourself in a bizarre (but somehow heartwarming) situation. At least you'll know we're all together on this ludicrous, tiring, but ultimately awesome journey of parenthood!

-Ryan O'Quinn

Infants

Rule #1

You will feel as though you will never sleep for eight hours again. Ever.

I remember the first three days my firstborn was on the planet. I paced the hallway thinking my wife and I were completely alone and there was no way humankind should have survived this long if parents got that little sleep! How was it possible? Would I ever get two hours straight again? Three?

Barring a miracle, eight hours is completely out of reach for the first nine months. The good news is that it gets better...eventually. Then kid #2 comes along and you start all over again!

Rule #2   You will be sure your kid is an alien.

On TV when babies are born, it takes about fifteen seconds of labor and the newborn is immediately handed to the mom, bundled up and beautiful. When babies are born in real life, they are wiggly, misshapen, odd-colored little creatures. Don't get me wrong, the first time you see your sweet angel is the greatest moment ever, but if we are totally honest, newborns look more like gooey aliens.

That kid on TV is not a newborn. The media has misled us! Not only does a real newborn look like an alien, that little guy has been in utero for nine months and somehow was able to manufacture poop from another planet.

You read about meconium in the books, but you never really expect the black gunk in the first few diapers to be that sticky, black, and just all around weird. What is that stuff? There is certainly a scientific explanation for this, but the adhesive factor of this substance is incredible. I scrubbed one rear end like I was removing rust from a bumper.

This sounds weird, but go with me on this: After the first few days of black alien-blob poop, it turns yellow and there is a "hot, buttered popcorn" smell until baby food is added to the diet. It will eventually dissipate, and you will miss it. Trust me, in just a few months, the foul stench that comes from a ripe Diaper Genie will make buzzards throw up.

Rule #3

You will always be too tired to read a book about getting your child to sleep because you have been TRYING TO GET YOUR CHILD TO SLEEP!

Everyone seems to have their own theories, ideas, wives tales, and formulas about children and sleep. You never know what will really work until you are standing in the hallway with your own unique, specific child. Most of the time during the infancy stage, the only thing you can think about is that magical moment years from now when you will actually get seven uninterrupted hours of sleep.

My wife and I had trouble with all of our little ones in the sleep department. That is not uncommon, of course, but having been one of the last of our friends to produce offspring, all of our contemporaries were on the other side of the sleep issue by the time we were going through it.

Our well-meaning friends offered countless aids and ideas to us and loaned us "amazing" and "helpful" books on how to get the tiny ones to snooze.

ARE YOU KIDDING ME?! Given a spare fifteen minutes in my day to actually crack open a book (other than this one), I had better be utilizing four minutes of that time to strip down and put on pajamas, three minutes to brush my teeth, four minutes to search the house in a frantic race to find where I have misplaced the baby monitor and four minutes to process everything that has happened in my day and immediately fall asleep.

By the way, those well-intentioned and possibly helpful books are all in a pile at our home. If you loaned them to us, please drop by and pick yours up. If you come over while I'm sleeping, don't wake me, but please feel free to stick around. You are now on diaper-duty.

Rule #4

You will look like a complete fool while trying to feed a child who is distracted by a toy, TV screen, or...anything.

Babies will simply not pay attention or open their mouths, and you will end up looking like a bouncing moron.

Pause for a second and look at what you are doing. You are bobbing and weaving while balancing pureed foods on a tiny spoon and aiming at a moving mouth target. At the same time, you are making sounds and opening your own mouth wider and wider in an attempt to get the little one to emulate your face and FOR THE LOVE OF ALL THINGS GOOD IN THE WORLD eat.

Meanwhile, your child is looking at the television behind you or out the window at something shiny. Good luck, fellow soldier. Good luck with the food, and the airplane game, and all the ridiculous things we do to keep these tiny people nourished. As long as you get at least some of this concoction into their mouths, you're doing just fine!

Rule #5

The first bite of baby food will ALWAYS be rejected.

Call it innate, natural, or just plain gross, but it is a fact of life and of science that the first bite of baby food inserted into the human child's oral cavity will be promptly forced back out. Following this disgusting eruption, the forsaken food will then go directly into that tiny crack between the bib and cute tee shirt that you have just changed for the second time in an hour.

The plastic baby food container with the peel back lid is hard to open. I look around for a candid camera every time I try to squeeze the container hard enough to hold it but not too hard to squish it. Then I pull the lid with enough force to peel it back but not too quick to spill the contents. If you've done this, you know what I mean. There is an art to the unnatural physics that must be employed to open this dreadful packaging.

No matter how careful you are, the food container will pop open and dispense a shotgun pattern of 7-12 bright orange droplets of sweet potatoes on your shirt regardless of where you aim the "weapon." You will end up changing your own clothes nearly as often as you change your child's. The ultimate example of cruel situational irony is the kitschy "Keep Calm" slogan on the front of the bib that is now covered with banana rice cereal and tears.

BONUS RULE:

At some point you stop changing your baby's clothes (and your own) and resign yourself to the fact that you will spend most of the day smelling like blueberry-spinach (yes, that is a real flavor).

BONUS BONUS RULE:

It's okay to taste the baby food. You may find yourself sampling those Stage 1 pears, sneaking bites of apple-squash-zucchini, or just trying a lick of the turkey-rice-carrot dinner to see if the combo really tastes as gross as it sounds...Ok, maybe that's just me, and now I've said too much.

Rule #6

You will accidentally talk to adults in a baby voice.

This is especially true when you have been with your kids all day long or generally find that you spend more time with your children than you do with adults.

I was in a drive-thru line recently. After I placed the order and drove around to get the food from the person at the window, I said in a slow, baby-like voice, "Awww, sweetie, that is so nice. Thank you very much for handing that to... (and this is where I heard what my own voice was saying, but it was too late)... Daddy."

Needless to say, I have avoided said establishment ever since.

Rule #7

"Out of the mouths of babes" becomes literal.

It's more than a Bible verse once you have your own adorable babe. My daughter takes this verse out of context every single day if I mistakenly offer her a bite of something new before she has swallowed her current bite. If I even get a new bite on the spoon, she will immediately expel her gob contents onto the floor in preparation for the next bite. This is where the family dog serves his primary purpose: cleaning up the piles of half chewed food from around the house (See Rule #32).

Don't even get me started on what the floor looks like after our family leaves a restaurant. Maybe eateries should look into getting a dog? Until then, I just leave a generous tip as a gesture that says, "I'm so sorry!"

As kids get older, the rule transitions from spitting out food to leaving food items around your home. I once found a petrified cheese quesadilla in my daughter's play kitchen that I could have used as a ninja throwing star.

Rule #8

You will often have soggy bits of food crammed into your mouth.

If anyone would have said this to me before I became a parent, I would have said, "No way!" I'd seen parents and children and the nasty things they did with food.

Children are selfish by nature and we spend much of parenthood extolling the virtues of sharing. However, when it comes to babies and soggy crackers, the selfishness goes out the window, and all they want to do is offer it to you. Unfortunately, they shove it in your mouth after it has come directly out of theirs.

I wouldn't have imagined it happening to me, but like many other things, I fell victim to the squeals of delight. Once your little cutie loses her breath laughing at you every time she forces a slimy graham cracker in your mouth, I guarantee you won't mind it nearly as much.

Rule #9

There is a finite amount of time between drying a baby off after a bath and the moment when she will pee all over your bed.

Cute little naked baby tushies are perfect for pinching, giggling about, and putting in an Anne Geddes calendar, but this admiration is short-lived. Your little angel will make you scream "NOOOO!" when she pees all over your fresh, clean bed sheets just at the moment you are reaching for a diaper.

For boys it is not necessarily your bed sheets that are at risk, but anything within a ten foot radius. The wall, your hamper full of clean clothes, or your open mouth as you shriek. You have been warned!

BONUS RULE:

The thread count of the sheets on your bed is directly proportional to the length of time it will take a little one to urinate when placed on your bed. Also, the more expensive the comforter, the higher the volume of pee that will soak through the comforter, sheets, and all the way to your mattress.

Rule #10

You should risk waking up a baby to change a full diaper.

In the middle of the night the last thing you want to do is wake your sleeping baby. Who in the world would do such a thing? They're sleeping. Let them be, right? Not necessarily - here is your dilemma:

1. Do you ride it out, leaving them in a soggy diaper, deciding not to wake your sleeping child and risk a blowout?
2. Do you try to head it off at the pass and change her while she is sleeping, hoping that your darling infant will not wake up during the diaper change?

If she has a full diaper in the middle of the night, she will probably wake up anyway. If you are awake and thinking clearly, you should go ahead and change her now, risking the interruption to sleep and what it could cause (i.e. baby wakes up for a few hours). I recommend this option not because I am a daredevil, but because some of the time, they do fall back asleep. It is much better for you to be fully awake changing a diaper than jumping straight out of bed to loud "change my diaper" screaming, then stumble, stub your toe, and have to rock her back to sleep in the dark while you are half awake.

More often than not, the reason she woke up is because of a blowout or seepage (a term I never used before kids). Either way, you are going to have to change the sheet and that requires turning on the light, which causes her to wake up and you are back to square one. I speak from experience.

Rule #11
Don't let those little bitty, tiny, cute and perfect fingers fool you. Your baby's fingernails will shred your face.

Your precious little angel will look at you lovingly, and will innocently grab your nose in childlike curiosity. Before you know it, they've clawed your face and left their mark: baby fingernail scratches! You thought they were going to paw your face like a tender kitten, but no. They have torn you up like a paper shredder.

It doesn't stop there either. Her cuteness will cause you to forget her destructive abilities as you allow her to put her hand in your mouth. She will laugh out loud as she scrapes your tongue with her fingers. Blame it on human nature, instinct, or some other insane baby phenomenon, but this kid can destroy human flesh in the blink of an eye. It is so funny to her, but you will look as though you were mauled by a wild animal.

Rule #12
You will start making practical arrangements to lop off your own finger in the middle of the night.

When your cute little bundle of joy has woken up six times in the last fifteen minutes and his only solace seems to come in the form of squeezing your index finger, you will fantasize about ways to take pruning shears and dismember yourself so you can leave the finger with him and go back to bed. Anything is worth another five minutes of shut-eye.

All sorts of crazy things run through the brain of a sleep-deprived parent. How do I invent a chair that will allow me to simultaneously sit and stand while rocking an infant? How can I patent a crib that is shaped exactly like an adult torso that will trick an infant into thinking he is being held all night long? I have a million of them...Patent pending, by the way, so don't get any ideas.

BONUS RULE:
Death, taxes, and this is certain: Upon successfully reinserting a pacifier in the middle of the night, your baby will wake up at the precise moment you get back in bed and are almost asleep.

Rule #13

When you are expecting a baby, you should diaper a dog while blindfolded.

I would suggest to expectant parents that they learn blindfolded diaper changing before the little one comes along, just to get into practice. Start with a baby doll, then work your way up to the dog. Yes, I diapered a dog. I have pictures. The dog was not happy, and did not sit still, which is exactly what made the whole event good practice for diapering real live human babies.

Sound crazy to wear a blindfold and diaper a dog? Yes. Helpful? Extremely. Let me explain:

When your child has a full diaper, you should change her despite the fact that she is sound asleep. (See Rule #10.) If you are mostly awake and already standing bedside, go for it. You also don't want to do anything to inadvertently fully wake her, which means you cannot turn on the light. You will need to master the art of changing a diaper in the dark for this reason.

If she wakes up during the change she will not be happy. Baby humans are not wired to sit still when someone else is putting clothes on them. Do whatever it takes to keep her asleep! Not unlike a restless puppy, she will wriggle her way out of a diaper in protest after realizing you are dressing her in the dark. There you have it: more reasons to practice diapering your dog.

If you have mastered dog diapering while blindfolded, you are prepared to both apply the diaper in the dark and do it on a mammal that may try to squirm away. You're welcome. I just bought you a few hours of sleep, and that's worth a lot to a parent.

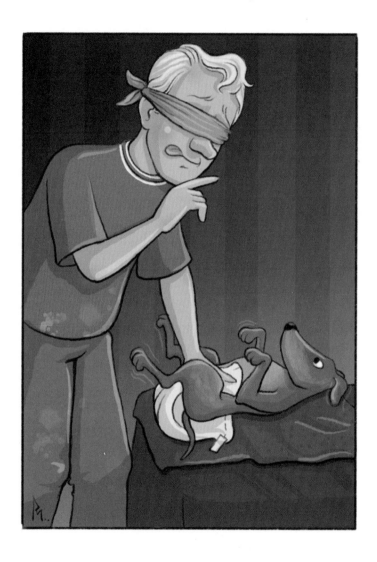

Rule #14

You will make a list of things to repair in the middle of the night.

This rule doesn't come into play because you have excess time on your hands. Let's be clear, when you're a parent there is none of that. List-making happens out of necessity. You are actually trying to figure out how in the world you can get more sleep.

One night after going into my infant's room numerous times to try and squelch the squeals, I slowly tiptoed out of the room only to have the creaking door send her into another round of uncontrollable sobs.

That's when the list began. I decided the moment I woke in the morning I would go around my domicile and repair anything and everything on the premises that could make noise, creak, squeak, slam, or grunt.

The things we parents think about in the middle of the night in our sleep-deprived stupor are comical to say the least. We are willing to go to any length, even massive home renovation, to get sixty more seconds of slumber.

Rule #15

You will completely freak out when the baby monitor coughs in your pocket.

Baby monitors are great. They are your eyes and ears while your sweet angel is drifting off to Sleepytown in their room. You will probably check it every ten seconds as they are first going to sleep. Seconds stretch into minutes and finally you almost forget about the monitor in your pocket.

At that precise moment, when you have all but forgotten that you have this device with you, your child will cough, sneeze, toot, or grunt and the monitor in your pocket will light up, vibrate, and scare the living daylights out of you. I suggest keeping it on a desk in a nearby room so you don't have to change your own underwear—your diaper pail is full enough already.

BONUS RULE:

Sometimes your baby monitor picks up the broadcast frequency from your neighbor's security camera. This happened to us. There is nothing that will cause you to panic more than checking in on your princess and seeing a live feed of the neighbor down the street watering his lawn.

Rule #16

Things that used to gross you out will not faze you at all.

There are a number of ways I could explain this rule to you, but I will offer just one example. It happened to me recently after a long night of trying to get my kids to sleep:

The butt paste was dangerously close to the toothpaste on the bathroom counter. I was just too tired to care. I'm pretty sure I grabbed the right one, but honestly I don't know. The extra two seconds that it would have taken me to bend my arm close to my face to examine the actual words on the tube and determine if it was meant for my baby's butt or my pearly whites would have been two more seconds I could've been sleeping. It wasn't worth it. I know it's gross, but you'll understand as you go along. You'll just be proud of yourself for remembering to brush your teeth at all.

Come to think of it, my breath is not as minty fresh as it used to be, but my gums are baby soft and I have a nice moisture barrier around my teeth and tongue.

Rule #17
You will poop with a kid sitting on your lap.

I can tell exactly who you are by how you just reacted to reading that last sentence. If you are expecting your first baby or are childless, you probably judged me and thought, "Gross! I will not." If you have been a parent for any length of time, you said in a calm voice, "Been there. Makes sense."

It's a strange phenomenon that can only be explained by the reality that your time is no longer your own. Period. You will constantly be interrupted regardless of what you are doing because you belong to someone else now. Shower time, potty time, sleep time: forget it. You are a cog in a machine that is bigger than you, and you will learn to wipe your butt with a kid on your lap. Why? Because you're a parent. End of story.

Rule #18
You will pee on your own foot in the middle of the night.

You may be thinking to yourself, "Yeah, right. I am a grown adult. I will not pee on any part of my body in the middle of the day or night." I'm not saying it will be a gusher, just a slight droplet or two that will be beyond your control.

Let me set the stage: You are exhausted, completely drained of energy. Your kid has not slept through the night in more than a week. You and your spouse have been at each other's throats about things like the proper consistency of rice cereal or the importance of matching baby shoes and onesies, when all you really need is a decent night's sleep.

All of a sudden, sometime in the middle of the night, you are roused from your slumber by high-pitched wailing on the baby monitor. In an attempt to keep your better half from waking up and the other kids from jumping out of bed—not to mention the neighbors from beating down your door—you race to the bedroom to console him.

You have scooped him up, rocked, kissed, and shushed him sufficiently when it hits you. "I HAVE TO PEE!"

There is nothing that you can do. You will have an armful of baby who is not yet asleep, and you can't go to the bathroom because you have no free hands. Despite your best efforts, at some point you will feel a teeny tiny trickle hit your foot. Guys, this is for you: I wear boxers. Now you know. Ladies, you will have zero control over the tinkle spigot. (Did I just coin a phrase?) You have been warned. One night you will pee on yourself and think, "That Parenting Rules book was right. I hate when Ryan's right."

Rule #19

Daddies, watch your nipples.

My wife has a great sense of humor and we have a lot of fun teasing each other. Throughout the breastfeeding months, I jokingly said that I was going to breastfeed the baby too just to get my wife to stop the "If you don't think it hurts, then you try it" talk. She dared me to try it so I could experience the excruciating pain she felt when little Junior sucked that nipple to the back of his throat in a millisecond. Rest assured, I never took her up on that offer. I decided she had every reason to complain if she wanted to, and I would bow out of the nipple-pain empathy match.

A friend of mine was having trouble getting their child to latch (another term I never used prior to having a child unless I was talking about a car part or an airplane fuselage). One day, the proud new papa was on the phone talking about the problems they were having with "latching." While on the phone, he was holding his baby, and this new dad did not have his shirt on. All of a sudden, the phone dropped and a bloodcurdling scream was heard on the other end. A minute or so later, he came back onto the line to report that Junior had decided to latch on to Daddy's now throbbing bosom!

BONUS RULE:

ALWAYS be nice to a breastfeeding woman. If you upset her, she will add cream to your coffee. This one requires no explanation. She carries life-sustaining weapons that can and will be used for evil when necessary. Enough said.

Rule #20

Your garbage cans will be full again two days after the trash truck has emptied them.

As I walk out to the curb each week, rolling the nineteen metric tons of filth that my home has produced in a few short days, I am shocked as I look up and down the block at the cute, tidy little cans that are neatly aligned along the picturesque, tree-lined street. I realize these precious retirees with their one (ONE!) little trashcan have just a few magazines and some apple cores to toss. I, on the other hand, have ordered extra garbage cans that line the sidewalk like a plastic barricade in front of my home, teeming with diapers from every corner, forcing the lid open and threatening to shower the pavement with our trash.

If you're one of those cloth diaper people who is totally disgusted reading about my trash cans of diapers filling our landfills, good for you. It is a noble endeavor you have embarked upon. Now, back to my blatant disregard for the environment.

Buy diapers in bulk and use your neighbors' cans after they go to sleep.

Rule #21

You will wish you had kids ten years earlier than you did.

I realize that this statement is a bold one, and perhaps you had your kids really young and can't relate. But if you are like me, your knees and ankles occasionally creak and pop like a former NFL linebacker. This becomes a problem as you get the wee one down to sleep for the fourth time and attempt to float out of the room without making a sound. At the most inopportune moment, a thunder crack sound from your ancient osteo parts will trigger your sleeping infant into a screaming rage.

The tricky part comes when you have finally coaxed Junior back to a peaceful slumber and are standing crib-side trying to figure out how to physically exit the room without walking. Sometimes it is just too risky.

Rule #22

Babies may actually be tiny research scientists.

Sometimes when babies are "dropping" something on the floor and looking so innocent and helpless waiting for you to pick it up, I am convinced they are actually conducting an experiment. I suspect they are trying to see how many times you will retrieve said object and hand it back to them. They probably report their findings to a scientific panel who is calculating how quickly we, the parents, are losing our minds.

I'm pretty sure I saw tally marks made with Cheerios on a high chair tray as I retrieved a baby spoon for the ninth time. More research to come.

Rule #23

You will be out in public without a child in your arms and find yourself swaying to and fro as if you are putting a baby to sleep.

Have you ever been on a boat, gotten onto land, and still felt like you were swaying back and forth with the movement of the water? It's the same with rocking a baby. Sometimes you just can't stop. Most people will look at you with a raised eyebrow and think you have lost your marbles. Sometimes you may catch yourself doing this, but most of the time you will not.

Let's all make a pact right now: The next time you observe parent-sans-baby-rocking, walk up to your fellow parents and gently whisper to them, "the baby is not in your arms." You will be appreciative when it happens to you, and we'll save each other from all kinds of public embarrassment.

Note: At other times you may find yourself swaying to and fro because these kids have caused you to genuinely lose your marbles. In this case, feel free to flag another parent over to rock with you. This way people will think you are both privy to a new exercise fad and wonder why they're out of the loop.

Rule #24

You will become a proponent of the No Restroom Left Behind movement, believing all bathrooms shall have equal standards, or at least equal changing tables.

I am a man. I have changed my fair share of diapers. Unlike my father before me, who changed his first diaper when I made him help with my daughter's Crap Fest (explained below in Rule #29), the dads of my generation are not afraid to get our hands dirty in this way. We're hands-on parents through the good, the bad, and the smelly.

Considering that my wife changes diapers all day long when I'm not home, I usually offer to take the stinky offspring to the men's restroom when we have a Stage 3 at a restaurant. More often than not, there are no changing tables in there. I'm not complaining too much, because selfishly this affords me the excuse to return to the table with "noxious butt" in tow, handing her to my scowling wife who just got diaper duty by default.

I have done my share of the ol' "standing diaper change" and it's not fun for anybody—parent or child. So allow me to make a public service announcement: ATTENTION restaurants, department stores, and amusement parks: Put changing tables in your restrooms, and don't forget that men are parents, too!

Rule #25

There are times when you will do anything to get your child to just go to sleep.

When my second-born child was nine months old, she went through a phase where the only thing that would make her go to sleep was if I stuck her entire baby fist into my mouth while holding her. For some reason this seemed to pacify her to the point of allowing her to drift off to La La Land.

Rule #26

It is sometimes physically and scientifically impossible to get the second leg into pajamas without the first one coming out.

We can put a man on the moon, cure diseases, and build skyscrapers, but we have not mastered the art of putting on baby PJs. I would venture to assume that for centuries humankind has been baffled by the mystery of the escaping leg. Mommies can multitask with the greatest of ease, and daddies can efficiently man the grill and watch the game, but we still have not mastered the art of putting two tiny legs into a pair of tiny pants.

Perhaps it's true that children are innately programmed to be naked. Maybe their little cartilage-y legs defy simple engineering, or possibly our adult brains just can't figure it out. Either way, despite our best efforts, those little legs shoot out of the pajamas, swimsuit bloomers, or pants before we can blink.

Rule #27

Your fourteen-pound princess can, and will, get you sick.

One week both my girls were sick at the same time. They were running a high temperature, had snotty noses, and generally felt awful. I thought because they were so small, there was no way that those little bodies could spread their germs and make a full grown man sick. They might have made each other sick, or made another small person sick, but I was healthy and taller than my kids. I was immune to baby people germs, right? Wrong. Baby germs are just as powerful. They will make you sick, so wash your hands and don't put their pacifier anywhere near your mouth—even to hold it there for a moment when you need two hands (my mistake)!

I told my wife recently that I felt like I was getting sick. She asked me how I knew. Here's how I knew: one of my ill kids sneezed directly into my open mouth, firing droplets of virus into my tonsils with laser-like precision, and I felt it happen. A day later, I was a full grown man sick from powerful baby germs.

Rule #28

Babies have a better altimeter than aviation equipment ever will.

I don't know how they do it, or why, but babies always know that you are trying to lie them down in a crib. I don't care if you have rocked that child until your arms are about to fall from the sides of your torso and your child has been passed out sleeping for two hours—the moment you start to lower their bodies, they spring forth with a violent scream that wakes up everybody in the house.

We need to somehow harness this amazing power and use it in military-grade aviation equipment. It doesn't matter if you have perfected the art of "baby lowering" without changing a millimeter of their pitch and yaw, the moment the innate altimeter is alerted, they are immediately awake.

Rule #29

You will do disgusting things you thought you would never do.

You will identify gross smells in crowded places in record time. Scenario: You're out in public in the midst of a crowd of strangers. Your refined olfactory sensors receive an alarm that a familiar scent is in the air. There is a foul aroma that indicates one of many scenarios originating from the same location. You then scoop up your kid in a busy mall food court or grocery store and in one motion, hoist him in the air to nose level and take in a long, deep sniff. With impeccable instinct, you can determine whether or not it was a toot or a poop and the degree of poopiness.

Stage 1: Turd Nugget
You will be able to continue shopping for at least another twenty minutes until you can get through the produce section.

Stage 2: Brown Pie
This will raise the threat level a bit, but your primary concern at this point is for other parents who might give you the stink eye (literally) when they walk past your family and catch a whiff. You have a few more minutes to complete your shopping until you need to resolve the issue.

Stage 3: Crap Fest
You are millimeters away from the bad stuff crossing the threshold of the elastic barrier in the diaper that will send you scrambling for another change of clothes. Stage 3 means you leave your shopping cart where it is and run to the closest restroom, alleyway, or janitor's closet to avoid the stinky ooze that ruined your last trip to the store by getting on your new shirt. And his shirt. And the groceries.

BONUS RULE:
You will eventually be able to change a poopy diaper and eat a Nutella crepe at the same time without flinching.

Toddlers

Rule #30
When your baby starts eating solid foods, those cute little "toots" become lethal.

Remember just a few months ago when it was cute? (See Rule #3.) It doesn't matter if your princess is sporting precious pigtails with pink bows while wearing an Easter dress, she will rip one that could make a chili-loving truck driver run from the room begging for mercy.

Kids do not inherently know that toots are funny or even stinky. It is just a natural bodily function that has happened since they were born. Children learn all the reactions that we have assigned to toots from us.

By the way, instead of toots there are other nouns for this duty, er...action, but we just say toots in our house. Poots are also acceptable. Fluffs is another one. One day after school, my five-year-old daughter, unintentional with her phrasing, let us know that she knew "the f word." My wife and I both froze. We carefully questioned her about the word, and she cupped her hand, leaned forward and whispered "fart" as if it were the worst thing she could ever say. Whew!

My suggestion is that you just let your kids naturally do their business as long as you can without flinching from the sound or stench. The moment my kids got a reaction from me, they tried to then force it out to make me cringe. Let's just say that exerting pressure on these stink bombs is not the way to go. That's a totally different rule that is covered next.

Rule #31

Sometimes the refried beans on your one-year-old's face are not refried beans.

I think you already know where I'm going with this one, but if it ever happens to you, it may make you gag and nearly swerve into traffic.

We were on our way to a comedy show that I was doing in Orange County, California. Since it was close enough to drive down the freeway from Los Angeles and come back the same night, I brought the whole family. On the way, we decided to pull in to a Mexican restaurant drive-thru to grab a bite for the road.

We placed our order, grabbed the food, and a few minutes later were back on the road. Just a couple minutes after that, I glanced in the rearview mirror and spotted some refried beans on the baby's face. At about the same time, my wife noticed it and we instinctively thought it was delicious Mexican fare that simply needed to be wiped away. Neither of us were alarmed, until we realized the bag of Mexican food was still sitting between us. We had not passed out the food yet! We both started screaming. I swerved to the side of the road.

I pulled the little one out of the seat and tried to figure out where to start. Our sweet baby had apparently decided to reach into her own diaper to check out what was happening in there. Sure enough, it was a dirty diaper and she thought it best to just pull her now-soiled hand out of the diaper and go about the business of painting her face, brushing the hair out of her eyes, and playing with her pacifier.

After a change of clothes and alternating screaming and gagging, we finally got back on the road. I'm pretty sure neither of us has eaten refried beans since.

BONUS RULE:

It will be times like this when you realize that you have exactly two wet wipes left in the diaper bag and you need to strategically wipe, fold, and wipe again and again and again. Like the story of the fishes and loaves, it is amazing how far we parents can stretch a single wipe or a tiny shred of a napkin when we have no other choice but to rely on miracles!

Rule #32

You will need a dog. Not for love and companionship, but to clean the mess under the table after your kids eat.

You will realize what real slobs you and your family are only after your dog goes to visit grandma for a few days. This happened to us.

After returning from family vacation, it was another couple of days before we had time to go retrieve the retriever. In the pup's absence, there were crumbs and food pieces everywhere. I finally realized why he never eats his dog food. He doesn't need to. He stays stuffed with the scraps that fall from my kids' hands and out of their mouths.

I spent most of my day picking up cereal puffs and cracker bits. It was then that I determined the family dog was more than a cuddly, playful creature; he had an essential role as our faithful vacuum cleaner. Sort of like a broom with a personality. A mop with a heartbeat. A paper towel with a flea collar. Somebody stop me.

Rule #33

Blocks of time can be measured in Cheerios.

One of the most difficult things for me to do is multitask. My wife says it is because I don't listen well. She says it's a guy thing and we don't pay attention. This can't possibly be the case. She also says...uh...she says something else about this, but I can't think of what it is right now.

At any rate, my wife is amazing at multitasking. When I prepare dinner, I have to boil the water, then add the pasta, then put that in a bowl and place it on the table, and then start the veggies. My brain just won't allow me to juggle everything the way my wife's does. I have no idea how she magically makes every part of the meal ready at the same time.

Trying to keep a child busy while you prepare dinner, clean the house, go to the bathroom, or anything else that requires you to have at least one hand free, is just a lot to ask.

I have found a solution. One of the best ways to do this is to dump some Cheerios on a tray. Parents have been doing this since General Mills created the breakfast food/parenting aid in 1941. These magical little Os are marvelous, but are also finite in their effectiveness as the hourglass sands dissipate and each little Cheerio disappears into their mouth: crunch, crunch, crunch, tick, tick, tick.

If you're like me, you'll glance over your shoulder from the kitchen, counting Cheerios and continuing to speed up your work as you see them dwindle.

There is a scientific measurement to this process—as each Cheerio lasts about four seconds—but the accuracy of that measurement is amended as the child's hands get bigger, the mouth gets wider, and they are able to cram more in their jaws. When figuring out how much time you need to buy with Cheerios, you must also account for the ones that will be discarded to the floor as your child tries to pick them up off the tray and shove them in her face.

To summarize, twenty Cheerios equals about forty seconds. Calculate accordingly, but don't overfeed. That'll require a totally different rule that involves industrial solvent, a mop, and maybe an invitation for the dog to come back inside.

Rule #34

You will drink from a sippy cup in public.

You will be in the car when it hits you. You are very thirsty and need a drink of something. Stat.

There is no fast food joint in sight, but you have been listening to that sippy cup roll around in the floorboard behind you for the last eleven miles.

While driving, you reach your hand back, grab a hair bow and drop it, grab half a chicken nugget and drop it, grab a Sunday School drawing from last Mother's Day and drop it, and finally grab the sippy cup. You raise it to your lips and pull with all the force of an industrial vacuum trying to quench your thirst. Mark my words, at that moment you will likely roll up to a traffic light, look to your left with the Dora the Explorer-emblazoned drink dispenser firmly on your lips and make eye contact with an old lady looking directly at you, eyebrows raised. I speak from experience.

Don't sweat it. You are a parent. That's what we do. Drink up!

BONUS RULE:

I'm a connoisseur of high pulp orange juice and the tiny holes of today's sippies do not work well with this drink. My kids whined and complained that the cup did not work for orange juice. I gave it a shot myself and discovered that low or no pulp works best. You can have your pulp back in a couple years when everyone has graduated to a real cup.

BONUS BONUS RULE:

You may have the urge to take a drink from a sippy that you find sitting around the house just to see how old it is. It's always good to do a smell test before you sip. Sometimes the sippy cup has been sitting around longer than you remember. Hopefully I've just saved you from chugging chunky milk.

BONUS BONUS BONUS RULE:

When your three-year-old says, "Come here and smell this, Daddy. I don't think it's chocolate milk," it's best to just leave it alone.

Rule #35
Your independent kid will want to repeat everything you try to do for her.

You've just gone ten rounds with your determined toddler who absolutely must do everything herself. You have hollered, struggled, and just pulled the last stitch of clothing over her nakedness when she defiantly strips everything off and starts all over. "Why?" you may ask, in a logical adult voice. It's simple. She wants to do it herself. She will therefore start from the beginning so she can put all of her clothes on again. All by herself.

By the way, this rule applies to other things, too. Including, but not limited to, getting back in the car and re-buckling in order to unbuckle herself and get out of the vehicle. All by herself.

As I'm writing this book, my daughter just asked for a drinkable yogurt from the refrigerator. I got up and got it for her. Then, I watched as she promptly put it down, spent a full minute dragging a chair across the room, climbing up on the chair, opening the fridge and getting one herself. Are you serious?!

The moral here: Just go with it and allow for more time than you had planned to do EVERYTHING. I'm sure smarter people than I will explain that this behavior is necessary for many psychological and developmental reasons, but nonetheless it is super-annoying. You are not alone. This is normal.

Rule #36 Whining is the best form of torture.

There is something special about the way toddlers communicate. They have a knack for making the words "why" or "no" multisyllabic. That screechy, nails-on-a-chalkboard sound that comes from their little whiny mouths is enough to make the hardest criminal break after a few hours alone in a room with one single toddler.

Admittedly, my wife has much more patience in this department than I do. This is how she communicates with them day in and day out. She understands that whining is almost like a dialect. It's just how they talk. Once you understand this, it makes the annoyance slightly more tolerable.

Still, I stand by my assertion. Put a sleep-deprived toddler in a room with someone that is not used to the sounds they make, and they will do anything to make it stop.

Rule #37
When you walk into any home, you will start to baby-proof everything.

As a parent your automatic, machine-like internal computer kicks in and you scan and survey the location. If I could describe it to you with a visual, imagine looking out of the Terminator's eyes as bits of data start scrolling up your screen to scan and evaluate the potential hazards in the immediate vicinity.

Within the first minutes inside my own father's home, I put some scissors in a drawer, pushed the television further back on the dresser, poured out a glass of old milk, and stuck some loose change in my pocket.

Everything becomes a potential hazard and the older the person you are visiting, the further removed they are from worrying about whether or not that safety pin or medicine dropper is in arm's reach of your toddler.

Rule #38
Outgoing text messages will often look like this: jj78eyj34yy7yjhkmn,h

Kids are just as fascinated with technology as parents. Once they discover that they can press a button, make something happen, and it makes interesting sounds, all bets are off. They'll take your cell phone, turn their backs to you as you try to snatch it out of their hands, and run in the opposite direction. This is typical modern toddler behavior, don't be alarmed.

You may occasionally be tempted to use your iPad, iPhone, or other screen to virtually babysit your child for a long period of time, but that is not healthy for either of you. The best thing to do in this situation is teach them how to use it properly and with moderation. My two-year-old asks if he can play with the iPhone, then turns it on, unlocks it, scrolls to the educational games, and starts playing one with no problem whatsoever.

When your toddler is given unsupervised carte blanche with your smartphone, awkward things can happen. Your boss will respond with a single question mark after "you" have texted her seventeen consonants in a row as a response to her question about tomorrow's presentation at work.

Rule #39

You will have in-depth conversations with your spouse about poop.

You don't set out to have these conversations. Let's face it, when you were dating your sweet betrothed, you never thought you would seriously speak these words. You probably also never considered you would discuss this topic for such a long period of time, nor be serious when you discuss it, but now that you are a parent, you definitely will.

My wife and I recently had a nearly ten-minute discussion about the firmness, texture, and consistency of our child's bowel movement. I don't know why it matters, but for some reason it does. Perhaps it's some sort of internal pride or a sense of parental enlightenment. Maybe it's just part of the general "this is what you missed today" information you communicate to the other party. Either way, you will feel the need to let the spouse know about it and if you don't volunteer the information, they will probably ask. Let's face it, when you are a parent, poop is important.

Rule #40

You will run toward the puke.

Prior to having children, I would nearly barf at the thought of anyone else upchucking in my vicinity. Before kids, I was the first one out the door when there was a hint of a gag. When you become a parent, something happens. A switch flips inside you and you are constantly prepared to catch puke.

Perhaps it's because at the first hint of a baby burp everything freezes Matrix-style and our now transformed "parent brain" flashes forward five minutes post-puke. You envision yourself on hands and knees scrubbing vomit off of the carpet and you want to preempt the strike. For this reason, I now find myself lunging across the table with my hands cupped under her chin at the slightest notion of warm, runny puke.

#WouldntHaveDoneThisAFewYearsAgo

Rule #41

If you have multiple children, you will count it a small miracle if they take an afternoon nap at the exact same time.

It is a rare occurrence, like Halley's Comet or winning the lottery, but every once in a great while the stars will align and your boisterous rug rats will actually take a nap simultaneously. The silence is nearly deafening because it is such an uncommon sound in your home.

This phenomenon, however, is not without complication. It is so rare and unfamiliar that you will find yourself literally not knowing what to do. Do you finish that TV show that has been paused for a week and a half, pick up the book you started while you were pregnant, try to squeeze in a workout, or do you try to...never mind...one just woke up.

Rule #42

You will prematurely rejoice before you discover that your child's early bedtime was really just a late nap.

The plans you made for the evening with your other half just went out the window as the clock strikes ten and Junior is singing at the top of his lungs, dancing on the sofa. "What do you want to do now, Mom and Dad!?" his dance seems to ask. That nap fired him up for round two of the day and now tomorrow's schedule will be completely thrown off, too. Greeaaat.

Before we had children, I assumed that they would sleep eight to twelve hours a night and no matter what time you put them to bed, they would just stay there for the duration and everything would shift accordingly. SO not true. Talk about a rude awakening!

Once in a great while you will meet a parent who has the miracle baby that falls asleep when they are supposed to and wakes up when you want them to and life is grand. But for the rest of us with human children, that is just not the case. They are on their own schedule with their own alarm clocks and their own agenda. They have absolutely no regard for your schedule, your day, or the fact that you actually planned to be asleep at 2:15 a.m.

Rule #43

You will be annoyed when people compare their pets to your human children.

I understand how people love animals. I have had a pet all of my life and I consider them precious little creatures that are entrusted to our care. However, take note: when I say, "My son was up all night screaming and then woke up at 5:30 a.m.," please do not say to me, "I know what you mean! Our Springer Spaniel tossed and turned at the foot of the bed last night."

You probably don't need a baby monitor on Fido and I can't turn Junior out to the side yard to do his business. It's two different things, people. My apologies for the soapbox, but when you set up a 529 college savings plan for your schnauzer and buy him a plane ticket to go see Aunt Loretta, then we can talk. Until then, just let me vent for a couple minutes...then you can go complain to your dog about me.

Dogs can be a good warm-up for any couple considering the idea of starting a family, but it is just not the same thing.

Rule #44

You will fondly remember the days when "sleeping in" didn't mean waking up just after seven a.m.

One of our single friends casually mentioned sleeping in on a Saturday and somehow inserted the detail that he woke up at noon.

My wife and I had just celebrated sleeping in also, but that meant our kids didn't wake up until seven. Remember what I said about everything changing? It's true. It's also true that morning snuggles with your kids are awesome. There is a tradeoff, which makes the early rising much more palatable.

Likewise, "staying up late" takes on a whole new meaning. I remember the days when my wife and I were newly married. We would stay up late and even leave the house to go out at 10 p.m. for crying out loud. Not anymore. Once we get everybody's pajamas on, teeth brushed, prayers said, tuck-ins complete, and start to talk to each other like adults for the first time all day, we are barely able to keep our eyes open. I rarely make a plan to see a film after eight. What's the point? I can stay home and sleep for free. By the time ten o'clock rolls around, I am useless.

Rule #45

You will amaze and baffle bystanders as you accurately translate toddler babble.

I have said it before, but parents have special abilities. One of the unexplainable talents is the ability to decipher exactly what your toddler is saying. To other people, it will make absolutely no sense at all. However, because you live with this little person day and night, you are accustomed to their tone, inflection, dialect, regionalism, and funny words.

Friends, neighbors and even grandparents are amazed as your little one says something that sounds like, "Ine choo cowy downy sepps." Without missing a beat, you will immediately say, "You want me to carry you down the steps?" Impressed onlookers may not clap, but they will want to.

BONUS RULE:

Sometimes you will misunderstand what toddlers are trying to say and it will be hysterical. I had a VERY long and confusing conversation with my two-year-old until I realized he had mixed up the words "elevator" and "alligator."

Rule #46

The only parents that don't have stains on their clothes have done one of two things: either abandoned their children, or hired a staff of nannies.

It is inevitable. You will get soiled. I remember being a childless person (that is the politically correct term I think) who was concerned with the occasional spot on my shirt or ink blot on the jeans. I used to sneak home for a quick change so that no one would notice such a terrible misrepresentation of all that I stood for as a person. Not anymore.

If you have small children, you will get messy.

More often than not, there are chocolate stains on my legs, spit up on my collar, or yogurt on my shirt. I no longer get upset or grossed out. I know it's going to happen and prepare myself accordingly. I don't go out of my way to change my clothes. I wear my messy clothes as a badge of "hands-on parenting" honor.

Rule #47
There will be all kinds of ways to accomplish simple tasks and sometimes they just look weird.

Have you ever seen an action movie where three or more people have their guns trained on each other? This is known as a Mexican standoff. Person A is pointing a gun at person B who is pointing at person C who is pointing at person A. You get it.

Sometimes child rearing is like that. We were once in a pizza restaurant and the baby was crying and only wanted me to hold and feed her. I had no arms free. The only way for me to eat was for my wife to slice little pieces of pizza and feed them to me on a fork. Catching on to the routine, our two-year-old started feeding my wife as my sister-in-law fed the two-year-old.

Rule #48

Your kid will be a detail-obsessed director that meticulously lays out every aspect of play time and story time.

I love making up stories with my kids and improvising. It started back when I would tuck my daughter in and tell her a story at bedtime. It seemed like no matter what story I attempted to tell, she had a better idea about how it should go. There were always different characters; they were doing different things, and she knew exactly the story she wanted to hear and exactly how it should be told.

Like any rational person, I said, "Well you just go ahead and tell the story." Nope. Not acceptable. She would have none of it. She wanted me to tell the story, and not only that, she wanted it repeated exactly like she had dictated it to me thirty-seven minutes ago when she started explaining how the story was to go.

I also get this sort of treatment when we are playing. There is always a storyline to everything we do. A playing session usually involves laying out the entire story arc of what we are about to play before we even start. This also includes dialog that will be exchanged and actions that will take place. Imagine watching a movie trailer for play time before you ever start playing. And, by the way, sometimes you never even get to the playing part. You just spend twenty-five minutes talking about what you are going to play and then move on to something else.

Rule #49

Forget about plot and storyline when it comes to playing with a toddler.

If you are really concerned about the machinations of a strong protagonist, a central premise, and resolving conflict when you are trying to play with a three or four-year-old, you are probably not going to have a very good time.

The children may have a good time, and that's the important part, but many of the conversations go like this:

"'Tend like you saw me but you didn't, and then you did, but you heard me and I didn't know....'"

This rule also goes hand-in-hand with the rule above that not much playing ever gets done. Three and four-year-olds would make excellent Hollywood executives. They are very accustomed to telling people what to do and if something finally gets done, it takes a long time to do it.

You've heard the old adage, "Hurry up and wait"? That's exactly what it's like trying to play with a toddler. There's a lot of set up, a lot of talking, and a little action that usually makes no sense in the grand scheme of what you were just playing. Bottom line: just go with it. They are only going to be this little once. Savor it and let them chart the course of the scene. Just play along.

Rule #50

Semantics matter.

It was snack time at our house. When my "snack presentation" was met with screams and cries, I was very confused—and so was my two-year-old. I could not figure out what in the world was going on. She had asked specifically for some food, and I met the demand.

I asked her to settle down and use her words. By the way, I never told anyone to use their words before I had children. Anyway, we simultaneously discovered that there was a semantics issue at play. She had confused the words pretzel and pickle. Snack time was not what she had expected or hoped for. I quickly remedied the issue and all was well again.

Clarifying has become a common practice in our house so that we don't end up with toes instead of toast or makeup in lieu of cupcakes. I've heard all of those.

Terrible Twos

Rule #51 Two-year-olds will cause you to yell, grab your hair with both hands, and regrettably wail, "Please. Stop. Talking!"

I have also dubbed this occurrence Purple Straw Syndrome. One day, I fixed my two-year-old some chocolate milk. She cried because she didn't want it in a sippy cup but preferred a "big girl cup." I obliged. Then she wanted a lid followed by a straw. When I had accomplished all of the above, she stomped her feet and cried while screaming, "Not that straw. I want a purple one!" When I accommodated that request she squealed, "NOT THAT PURPLE STRAW!!" I took a deep breath, screamed inside my head, and calmly walked away.

Welcome to the terrible twos. Someday if you find me in a corner rocking and whispering, "not that purple straw..." you'll know that I just went through one too many "terrible two" years.

Rule #52

The sincere prayers of a toddler are the sweetest sound this side of Heaven.

When my firstborn started talking, we began saying night-night prayers. My heart swelled up every time I heard her sincere little voice lift to Heaven and pray for little friends, the dog, and even distant relatives that I left out of my prayers. Her prayers were so innocent and amazing I couldn't help but burst with joy as she named everyone.

Like everything else in a two-year-old's life, prayers are a bit unpredictable. Sometimes they will be deep and poetic; other times they will be about cartoon characters, baby dolls, and the cashier at the supermarket.

Whatever is on their hearts, let them lift it up for as long or as short as they desire. God is listening no matter what they talk about.

Rule #53

Your kids will develop strange allergies.

Maybe I just haven't been paying attention, but it seems like everyone these days has some sort of allergy, whether it is dairy, nuts, gluten, soap, sugar, corn, hairspray...I could go on.

As it turns out, my kids are all allergic to wearing clothes! It does not matter if it's after a bath, time to go out in public, or a change following a spill, my kids will refuse to put on clothes. You can ask them nicely or try to reason with them and explain the consequences, but it usually falls on uncaring little ears.

This is the part where we have to pick our battles. As a parent, you will eventually reach an invisible threshold where you will question the need for humans to wear clothes at all because you are just too tired to argue with your children.

Rule #54

You will spell things aloud to other adults when you don't have to.

During one of my daughter's two-year-old phases, she would cry and demand a pacifier every time we uttered the "P word" out loud. She could be downstairs while my wife and I were whispering in our bathroom upstairs and she would hear us. If we said "pacifier," she would scream until we handed her one. It's not that we were giving in to demands. This is the "pick your battles" argument again where giving her a paci was much less painful than hearing her scream.

Like many generations of parents before us, in order to avoid conflict and screaming, we started spelling out words we didn't want a child to hear. This kind of behavior was addictive and we started spelling everything. We would definitely spell B-A-T-H. That eventually led us to spelling S-H-O-E-S and finally moving on to B-E-D.

After a while, we couldn't stop. We were on a roll. We were spelling things even when we didn't mean to. We didn't want to. It was just becoming natural. The more we spelled, the more we wanted to spell. OK. I exaggerate, but you get the point. You will spell things you don't have to in front of grown adults who can both read and understand the words you S-P-E-A-K.

Rule #55

You will see a five minute shower as a spa vacation.

One Saturday morning my wife announced, as she turned on the water for the shower, "I haven't showered since Tuesday." I smiled knowing that the brief few minutes to let the water run over her, uninterrupted, felt like a five-star retreat in these days of yogurt hair, Play-Doh fingernails, and crusty something on her arm.

My wife savored the shower time especially after she stopped bathing with our kids in the tub due to the possibility of spontaneous turd launch during bath time. (See next rule.)

Rule #56

When you have children, you realize that the human body is not equipped with enough limbs to accomplish the tasks you need to do.

I have seen my wife prepare breakfast while holding a six-month-old and a two-year-old. She somehow managed to scramble eggs with one hand, make sausage with another, pour orange juice with another, and wipe a face with another. The demand is great for every finger, elbow, and arm to pitch in and do their part.

My wife and I are learning the art of ninja parenting as we hold, comfort, cook, clean, organize, and prepare—all with two hands each. I'd give her a high five for her amazing skill and creativity accomplishing tasks the way she does, but my hands are full.

Nothing compares to the tender words "Hold me, Daddy." You will figure out a way to make it happen even if you are completely loaded down and juggling a dozen other things.

Rule #57

You will see whole kernel corn floating in the tub and it will take five-and-a-half seconds for you to realize what just happened.

See what I mean? It just dawned on you. When this happens, it is usually followed by a loud scream.

There are things you are warned about as you become a parent. You probably know there will be some messes. You know there are sweet cuddle times, tummy aches, and tantrums. However, nothing really prepares you for the brown log that floats up to invade bath time.

These Baby Ruth moments often come without warning and always ruin your whole night. There are three distinct kinds of stinky submarines, each one progressively worse than the last.

The first is the "I see my child giggle and spy the stinky visitor soon after launch" turd. This is followed by a scream on your part and a similar startled response by your offspring. You scoop him out of the tub and hit the drain lever in one swift motion.

The second type is the "I've finished the bath and see a Cleveland Brown after the tub has drained" syndrome. This is worse than the previous one because it means you have soiled the towel, your naked child who is snuggled to your bosom has fecal flecks on his person, and now you have to repeat the entire bath after scouring, bleaching, and scrubbing the tub again, which delays bed time by another half hour.

The third is the terrible "I'm in the tub with Junior during the squeeze session and we are both covered in doo-doo." This one involves the loudest scream of all, some running, usually a little spitting for some reason, and a redo of bath time. Nevermind. The bath is out. We're taking this do over in the shower!

Rule #58

You will secretly delay potty training because you're tired of stopping the car for bathroom breaks every three miles.

This rule is something you would never believe when you are elbow-deep in poop in the diaper-changing years. During the early diaper days you think to yourself, "One of these days I will never have to change diapers again."

The problem is when your toddler is three years old, she has the bladder of, well, a three-year-old. She will beg you to stop twice on the way to the grocery store, once on the way home, and probably in the garage while you are trying to get her out of the car seat.

Public bathrooms are the worst part of potty training. You now have to endure the frightening reality of the bathrooms at theme parks, rest areas, and highway gas stations.

The task will be: 25% getting her on and off the potty, 25% keeping her clothes precariously dangling around her ankles and not on the floor, and 50% screaming repeatedly, "Don't touch anything!"

BONUS RULE:

I have since learned that keeping a small or collapsible training potty in the back of the car remedies the above public bathroom problems. However, parents should not be tempted to use the tiny potty for personal relief. My wife tried it. It didn't end well.

Rule #59

Children are very literal.

I told our two-year-old to "wipe the chocolate from her face." She did exactly what I said and started on the outside of her face with a wet wipe. After moderate success in moving chocolate around, she opened up her mouth and started cleaning away all the chocolate inside her mouth, too.

General Rules

Rule #60
The Play-Doh folks must have stock shares in a carpet company.

If you have carpet anywhere in your home, it will become a Play-Doh magnet. I don't care if your entire house has hardwood, laminate, or tile. If there is a throw rug in the deep recesses of the closet, your kid will find it and get Play-Doh on it. I am certain there is a link between the two companies.

Rule #61
Sometimes sharing doesn't mean what they think it does.

Parents need to be specific about exactly what sharing is. When our good friends were in the middle of teaching their daughter about the concept, they took her to the doctor for a check-up. She walked straight to the toy area in the waiting room, violently snatched a toy away from another kid and screamed, "Share!" She almost had this sharing thing down. Back to the drawing board.

Rule #62

Uncrustables will ruin your diet.

When you have small children in your life, it is extremely difficult to get out the door for school, work, or church in the mornings. There are a few companies that have attempted to make our lives a bit easier.

If your household is like mine, there is an imaginary clock that starts ticking in the morning as soon as anyone wakes up. That clock is the ominous countdown clock that figuratively gets louder and louder the closer we get to the departure time, urging us to get out the door. Inevitably, there is yelling and running and it usually culminates in a parent running back inside at the last minute to grab a pair of shoes that one or all children have forgotten to put on.

These companies that I spoke of earlier are the fine folks that make the genius pre-packaged lunches that we can grab from the refrigerator and throw into a backpack or lunchbox rather than spend the extra four minutes to make a sandwich or cut some fruit. Four minutes may not sound like a lot, but when you are dealing with traffic, tardies, and tantrums, you will start factoring in milliseconds.

One notable company makes a delicious concoction called Uncrustables. This is the famous pre-made peanut butter and jelly sandwich. They are so delicious that I am certain that the company makes them for adults, yet tricks us into buying them for children. Our children rarely finish one of these sandwiches, thereby forcing my wife or me to eat the remainder, not letting such tasty food go to waste.

Mark my words: You can gain between seven and eleven pounds just by eating Uncrustables. I'm pretty certain the company that owns Jenny Craig also owns this company, and there is a giant conspiracy between the two. I'll do some research on this as well and get back to you.

Rule #63

A sense of humor is necessary for many reasons, including dinner party conversation about poop.

Once at a dinner party, my daughter said what was on her mind. The dinner conversation had not been about any topics related to biological functions nor the necessity of reading paraphernalia in said situation, but my daughter decided to exclaim aloud to everyone at the table, "Daddy if you need to go poop, I will bring you a magazine!"

The table laughed, I smiled, dropped my head, kissed my girl, and chose to be grateful for the thoughtful gesture.

Rule #64

If you have multiple kids they will fight over [insert ANY word].

Allow me to set the stage: One day while working in my home office on the second floor, I heard that all too familiar sound of escalating violence coming from the downstairs play room. It was the kind of sound that means someone is about to get punched, smacked, cut, or shot. I ventured into the family room just in time to see the four-year-old trying desperately to keep the three-year-old from getting the nothing she had in her hand. Yes, you read this correctly. She had an invisible cookie in her hand and was keeping it from the younger one who was crying.

The four-year-old took off running and made it to the living room just before she was tackled by her sister who promptly swiped the INVISIBLE cookie from her and ran the other direction.

The older girl caught up to her by the front door and they both rolled into it with a thud. The four-year-old took the cookie and held it above the little one's head. The little one was screaming, kicking, and crying over NOTHING.

After witnessing all of this with mouth agape, I did the only thing that a rational adult human male would do in this situation. I yelled, "STOP THIS! Follow me." Then, I walked into the living room, got down on my knees and "made" more invisible cookies! I distributed them evenly to each kid and had them go to separate rooms to "eat" them. I also made one for myself and it was delicious.

Rule #65
Kids will have unwinnable arguments.

Recently I heard an argument in another room that was starting to escalate to that point where parents actually have to stop everything they are doing to avoid more crying that is sure to follow if they don't intervene.

Children are often wise beyond their years and will floor you with life observations and mouth-dropping musings. This was not one of those times.

As I neared the end of the hallway and made my way into Princess Central (aka the girls' bedroom) this is what I heard:

Lilah: I LIKE PINK MORE!
Haley: I LIKE PURPLE MORE!
Lilah: I LIKE PINK MORE THAN YOU LIKE PURPLE!!
Haley: NO! I LIKE PURPLE MORE!!

Now my question is, as a reasonable parent, how do you explain the insanity of such philosophical rhetoric? Once again, I did the only logical thing to do and exclaimed in a matching tone, "I LIKE BLUE MORE THAN EITHER ONE OF YOU EVER WILL. NOW STOP YELLING!"

I'm pretty sure I am now somehow trained in the art of being a children's conflict mediator or maybe a S.W.A.T negotiator for people under five years old.

Rule #66

There will be a fight over elevator buttons.

I wish I could mass-produce elevator buttons and hand them out to every parent. This way they could just keep them in their front pocket or purse for every trip to a hotel when the need for them arises.

If you have more than one child, the moment you step outside of your hotel room there is a mad dash to the elevator that shames most Olympians. Regardless of who reaches the elevator first, there is always a shoving match, some yelling, and a rapid-fire button-pushing contest. In that order.

This is usually followed by a mom or dad, or both, yelling at all children involved to stop fighting, screaming, and pushing the button. The annoyed and embarrassed parent will then try to remedy the situation by offering sage wisdom in this way: the other child(ren) can push the floor number on the inside of the elevator once the door opens.

Note to parents: This has never worked in the history of humankind. The second the elevator door opens, there is another rocket-powered burst of running inside the door and some amazing basketball boxing-out technique going on that would rival NBA players. Therefore, I stand by my patent-pending idea to hand out elevator buttons and let parents give them out regularly to avoid the whole annoying ordeal.

Rule #67 You will probably have a chicken finger in your pocket.

Your children will ask you things, say things, and do things at the most inopportune moments. This is a broad stroke and general law of parenting, but just know that they will pick their nose in the restaurant, scream in front of the pastor, and ask you to hold something when your hands are obviously full.

The latter is a phenomenon that is best described with a story. My five-year-old recently asked me to hold something. It was my fault that I did not ask her to repeat the all-important noun in that sentence. So, I simply replied, "Stick it in my pocket."

Forty-five minutes later I realized that the "something" was a half-eaten chicken strip, and it had been sticking out of my front pocket since I instructed her to put it there. She was simply obeying me, and it was all my fault for not getting all the info. Could've been worse. It could've been covered in BBQ sauce!

Rule #68

You will choose a restaurant based on the quality of their pre-dinner crayons.

When you don't have children, restaurant outings are a nice, casual affair and something to look forward to. It is usually a delightful event that entails a bit of discussion with your significant other about where you will go, what you will choose to eat, and when you should leave the house to get there.

With children, all of these things go out the window and the outing is much more akin to a strategic military operation. Here are some considerations:

1. Where can we go that is moderately loud and we will not be judged by those sitting around us trying to enjoy their dining experience?

2. Is there a restaurant that often has food scattered on the floor? (See Rule #7.) I know this is going to happen, so I would like to go there to avoid the ridicule.

3. How far is the restaurant from home and how will that affect the nap potential factor? After 3 p.m. you must be very careful about how far you drive from your home because there is a dreaded possibility that the little one(s) will fall asleep in the car if it happens to exceed the NZR (Nap Zone Radius). Anything over twelve minutes one way in the car in either direction from your home after this time will make wakeups difficult and add two hours to normal bedtime.

4. How quickly will the servers bring food to my table? There is a meltdown period in any restaurant wherein offspring will get exceedingly bored with everything around them and commence freaking out. This can be temporarily offset by the quality of crayons and pre-dinner activities that are presented to you upon being seated. Mexican restaurants are usually quick and they often serve chips and salsa to avoid a pre-dinner tantrum. Restaurants that offer bread and butter can be a lifesaver when it comes to staving off the boredom factor that accompanies a toddler's visit.

Rule #69

You will check the pants.

Reading this rule you will probably assume that it has something to do with making sure Junior did not go #2 in his pants. Although that is definitely something you should and will check on a regular basis, this rule is referring to something different.

One night our family decided at the last minute to go out for dinner. For whatever reason we did not feel like cooking that evening and made a rush decision to get out the door and avoid the crowd at our favorite restaurant. With a family of five it is not easy to just walk out the door and get into the car.

We rushed as quickly as possible, gathered the kids, threw them in the car, and raced to the restaurant. When we sat down at the restaurant, my wife and I had a minor panic attack when one of us posed the question, "Do all of our kids have pants on?"

It was a real, legitimate, I'm-not-trying-to-be-funny moment and for a split second we literally didn't know if our children were currently wearing pants. We craned our necks under the table to be sure that all of our kids were clothed on the lower half of their bodies. When three pairs of pants were accounted for, then and only then, could we enjoy our dinner together.

If you're operating on two hours of sleep in the infant stage, you will check for your own pants, too. If you're nursing, you'll double check for a bra.

Rule #70

You will forget their shoes.

We could buy three new pairs of shoes a week with the gas money we'd save if we didn't go back home over and over to get our kids' shoes.

As you leave your home, especially when you are in a rush to go anywhere, you will experience these moments of insanity. If there is any sort of deadline or something that is starting at a specific time (school, dentist appointment, church, birthday party) you will absolutely have at least one time where you forget shoes, clothes, bottles, blanket, pacifier, or all of the above.

I really wish I had some wisdom to impart to you such as delegate responsibilities, or develop a system, or put things in the car the night before. Nope. Let me save you the trouble. Nothing works. Just resign yourself to the fact that you, like the O'Quinns, will find yourself in the parking lot trying to figure out how you can manufacture clothing on the spot. It will also involve you looking in the glove box. I don't know why we assume that once, in a moment of genius, we walked to the garage and said to ourselves, "One of these days I will need this pair of shoes, therefore I will hide them in the glove box for just such an occasion." This will never happen. Nonetheless, you will check just in case.

Rule #71

You may forget the baby.

I really deliberated whether or not to leave this entry in the book. After two of my friends reported the same incident, I decided there were either only three of us in the world that have ever done this, or it is a Parenting Rule. I went with the latter. We may as well come clean.

We were leaving the house one afternoon and as we started backing out of the driveway and discussing whether or not we had the baby's shoes, the five-year-old quietly reported that we had indeed forgotten the baby.

Before you start calling Child Protective Services on us, please realize that we didn't get far. We had just backed out of the garage before we were admonished by our oldest child that we had left our youngest in the house. Thank goodness for first born children! They think they know it all, and sometimes they actually do.

This will likely only happen if your children outnumber you and your spouse, but that is not a hard rule. Remember, pregnancy brain lasts a lifetime.

Rule #72
You can be too good at convincing your kid that a toy is awesome.

If you have multiple children, especially close in age, you will learn that teaching them to share is one of the toughest things to do. They will always want what the other child is playing with. As a parent you think, "Well, this is easy, I just have to make another toy seem so appealing that the screaming child will want to play with that one."

The trouble is, you can be too good at it, and both children will switch their loyalty to clamor for this newly hyped and awesome toy.

Once, I could not find Band-Aids for a cut on my daughter's finger. I convinced my two-year-old that a folded Kleenex attached with masking tape was a special Band-Aid designed for little princesses. She refused to take it off for two days. Even after we bought more Band-Aids she demanded that Daddy give her the special one and her older sister now only wanted "special" Band-Aids too.

BONUS RULE:
They will always want something else. We were in the backyard playing and I decided to pass the time (and tire them out) by having races across the yard. The kids naturally came across the finish line according to their ages. I was just about to give them each first place in their age divisions to avoid a younger sibling meltdown when the oldest screeched, "It's not fair! I want to be third place like Haley!" That's it. I give up.

Rule #73

It takes two-and-a-half hours to watch a twenty-two minute sitcom.

This has been tested over and over again with precision and accuracy. If your child is over twelve months old, you will inevitably be three episodes behind on your favorite DVRed shows. If you attempt to watch the show while any child is awake, it will take you a minimum of 150 minutes. You will constantly be interrupted by a spill, a fight, or the need to have a tickle war. (See Rule #91.)

If your kids are asleep, it is highly likely that eight minutes after sitting down for the first time all day, you will be too sleepy to do anything, especially watch television. If you love hour-long dramas, triple it and be prepared to spread that three hours of viewing time over the next two weeks!

Forget about watching a feature film at home for the next five years. Oh, and don't go to the movie theatre after 9 p.m. to see one either, unless you are super-excited about spending $11 for a couple hours of good sleep.

Rule #74

You will soon change the way you tell time.

Modern technology has made parenting easier on many levels. We can watch and talk to our kids via handheld monitors from another room. We can schedule feedings, order diapers, and make doctor appointments all from our smartphones.

Modern technology has altered the way we watch TV as well as the way we tell time. With the advent of the DVR, we have not had to watch television in real time for many years. I don't even know which days of the week the shows are on. I just press "List" on the remote control and scroll down to find what I want to watch. My kids have also learned the power of the remote and it has changed their dialog as well.

Recently, my five-year-old said something that I will likely adopt and repeat as my own. When I asked her to switch off the television she responded, "Can I just watch a couple more inches of this show?" She was referring to the scrub bar timeline at the bottom of the screen. Who knew you measure time in inches? Now you can.

Rule #75

Sometimes a child's logic is a bit confused.

My three-year-old had the hiccups. She was visibly upset by this fact because she couldn't complete a sentence without being interrupted by the annoyance. Having part of the information correct, she announced that she would go somewhere in the house and hide in the hopes that someone would come find her and scare the hiccups out of her.

Rule #76

You will now eat dinner at 5 p.m.

Continuing the theme of "everything changes," your daily routine will be drastically altered for a number of reasons. Keep in mind that bedtime is about four hours earlier than it was before you had kids. When this important shift happens, everything else moves accordingly and you will now find yourself eating dinner much earlier.

If you do venture out to a restaurant during this window of time, you will inevitably find two groups of people: those that seek out the senior citizen specials and those in search of "Kids Eat Free" menus. This is quite awkward as the people that usually have the least amount of tolerance for children (old folks gumming their Early Bird Special) are the only other folks in the restaurant, rolling their eyes and making faces at your unruly brood.

My first thought was that the restaurants should just segregate these age groups to different sides of the building, but then I realized that God, in His infinite wisdom, made old people not be able to hear very well—problem solved.

Rule #77

A two minute shower costs a lot.

I have been away on a trip or a comedy tour and returned to hear my wife say something like, "I haven't showered since Tuesday." Certain this is just a saying, I never believed her. Anyone can find time for a two minute shower, right? What's the big deal?

My wife went out of town recently and I decided to quickly jump in the shower. What could go wrong? I'm a dude. We are masters of the 120-second rinse. All the kids were occupied. No fighting. No crying. In fact, they were all in different rooms. I jumped in, showered quickly, jumped out and walked down the hallway to my son's room to find fourteen small paper cups of water spilled on his floor. Fourteen! How could this happen? Simple really. He took the step stool he uses for brushing his teeth to reach the little rinse cups, filled them up over and over and ran back and forth from the bathroom to his bedroom until fourteen of them were on his new carpet.

I get it, she wasn't bluffing. My wife really hadn't taken a shower since Tuesday. Sometimes a shower is just not worth it.

Rule #78

People who had children before you will always talk about how much easier you have it than they did.

Even if your sister-in-law popped out a kidlet three days before you, you will never hear the end to how much easier you have it and that she didn't have all these "new advancements." Okay, maybe I'm exaggerating, but not by much. Things are always changing. There's a new spoon, a new bouncer, or something that claims to make life easier. My mother-in-law was blown away by a pack-n-play. I think she also marveled at disposable diapers, but that's another story.

After our second child was born, we got a cool new double jogger stroller. Shortly into the life of the stroller we noticed a wobbly wheel. We went back to exchange it only to discover there was no such stroller on the market. The company had replaced it with a fancy new one that included a sleek new look, bigger tires, and an mp3 player. It would only cost me 400 bucks to get it!

The truth is new things may make parenting temporarily easier, but there are age-old parenting tools that no amount of technology or baby registry items can replace.

Rule #79
Counting backwards from five always works.

I don't know why or how, but if you have reached the end of your rope in asking kids to do anything, you can start counting backwards very loudly with authority and everything changes.

Like a Big Red Button you use only in case of emergency, you should use this fail-safe sparingly. Keep in mind it is not merely counting. That won't work. To use it properly you must count loudly and stare directly at the individual(s) to whom you are speaking with a hint of crazy in your eyes. A furrowed brow is helpful and as a bonus, you can hold your corresponding fingers up to underscore the urgency of the countdown.

I don't know that anyone really knows what happens when a parent reaches zero. I shudder at the thought. My wife is an absolute master at the countdown. All she has to do is start counting backwards and even I snap to attention...just like I did when I was five.

Rule #80

If you are out of the room the oldest child will assume the role of parent.

It is the natural order of things. Like a message from an after-school special, kids learn by watching you. They want to act like you act and do what you do, and the longer you are a parent the more you realize that those little rugrats start to sound exactly like you.

The most ridiculous things come out of their little mouths, and it is a verbatim replica of the ridiculous things that you say (or have said once upon a time). They have a steel trap for a mind, so don't think you can just say or do something one time and they will forget it. That is out of the question.

Older children relish the chance to parent their younger siblings and this can sometimes be sweet and innocent. Other times, it's an opportunity for plain old childhood mischief.

I walked out of my daughter's room and was just down the hall when I heard the older one say to her younger sister, "Taste this milk and see if it is old." I felt like it was a scene from a movie where I was running toward their bedroom in slow motion yelling NOOOOO! I reached the door just in time to see the one-year-old hoisting the old milk to her face and gulping as the three-year-old smiled knowingly.

My oldest child has also been known to say phrases like, "I am sick and tired of this," "Don't make me tell you again," and one of my all-time faves, "I am not playing. I have had it."

Rule #81

Sometimes you have to peel two bananas.

This rule could very well be the title of this book because it covers a multitude of rules. My incredibly intelligent wife often says "pick your battles" when it comes to our children.

Despite trying to do things logically and efficiently, such as getting one banana and cutting it in two for two children who will not eat a whole one, you will have to use two bananas and resign yourself to eating the leftovers.

When we had two children under three years old we learned the hard way that the best thing for a trip to Disneyland was to give them each their own baggie of Goldfish crackers, fruit slices, sippy cups, and every other sort of snack. Children (and adults) have a predilection not to share. It's human nature. We harp constantly in the pre-K years and beyond about the importance of sharing, but they just don't. The bottom line: You can either stick to your guns and fight or just peel two bananas.

Rule #82

Your children will diagnose themselves and treat the symptoms.

Kids are keenly aware of what is going on with them and their little bodies. They don't always understand why they get sick or what exactly is happening, but they do know something is going on.

Once, my three-year-old had a cold. She felt rotten but was savvy enough to know that when she felt this way she could not go outside or play and run around like she usually does. She came to me and quickly diagnosed herself, attempting to allay my fears and consequent squelching of her fun in one hysterical sentence: "I'm not sick today, Daddy. I can go play," she said. "I just have nose problems. When I breathe, my nose blows bubbles."

Rule #83

Given the opportunity to "sprinkle on a couple chocolate chips," your child will use both hands.

Luckily for me, my wife loves to cook. Since the moment she was barely tall enough to pull the kitchen drawers out and climb up the handles to sit on the countertop, she has been cooking. She has great memories about making meals with her mother and grandmother before she could reach ingredients in the refrigerator. It's for this reason that she allows our kids to explore the joy of cooking at a very young age.

It requires a great deal of patience to allow a tiny sous-chef in your kitchen that might have only just learned to sit on the potty. When you have a little helper on the counter, more often than not your chocolate chips will outweigh your cookie dough, the syrup will puddle on the French toast, and the brown sugar to oatmeal ratio will be approximately 7-to-1.

You can try to teach them the importance of using exact measurements when they are ready to learn, but in the beginning it may just be best to let them play and resign yourself to making a separate batch of cookies that doesn't contain eight cups of sugar.

Rule #84

You will need to invest in a good plunger.

Everybody poops (except my wife, I'm told). After more than ten years of marriage, I still can't prove that she partakes in this bodily function, but I'll save that for my next book. I prefer to continue believing this fairy tale until proven otherwise.

Kids are infatuated with poop, especially our little girls for some reason. When my oldest was potty training she would do it, then analyze it. She was blessed or cursed with a digestive system that would produce the kind of outcome that could make NFL players shake their heads in awe of what happened in that little potty.

More than once I've had to plunge the stubborn stuff. In fact, while I was away from home on a trip, my wife called to tell me we needed to buy an industrial plunger. Not just a plunger, mind you, but a commercial-grade-heavy-duty-built-to-last-hard-core piece of equipment.

You get what you pay for, and perhaps this should be on the list of things you put on a baby registry. It's something that you want other people to spend good money on — a practical tool you'll need in your home when they are big enough to use the "big potty."

The next time you're invited to a baby shower, bring a plunger with a bow on it. It may take the new parents a couple years to understand, but they will thank you.

Rule #85

Their keepsakes will be disgusting.

Apparently during a playdate, my four-year-old and her friend worked hard to extract an annoying booger from her nose. They were unsuccessful. The next morning, however, my daughter succeeded in her endeavor and removed the treasure from her right nostril. Her mining expedition was completed about one-and-a-half hours before preschool started, and she wanted to save it to show her friend who had tried to help her earlier.

She decided, in her practical preschool wisdom, to stuff the booger under her fingernail to keep it there until she could proudly display it to her friend. According to her, this way she could still eat her breakfast and not disturb the booger.

I'm glad she got to eat breakfast, because this whole escapade totally ruined my appetite.

Rule #86

Your children will occasionally be considerate.

As your children grow, their brains will expand. As their little brains expand, they will learn to talk. As they learn to talk, they will manage to tick you off from time to time with insolent remarks and selfish behavior.

Your children will also occasionally be considerate almost to the point that it is alarming and off-putting. As in, "What's your deal, little kid? I know you've got an angle here. I also know you are smarter than me, but I would never admit it, so why are you being this way?"

I was working in my home office when my four-year-old walked in and said in an angelic voice, "I have an itch on my back. If you get a chance at some point today, could you please scratch it for me?"

Her polite request and consideration of my time was almost worse than any yelling or deviant behavior. It was so unlike her usual appeals I didn't know what to make of it. I'm still waiting to find out what her angle was.

Rule #87

You may know every line of a Disney movie without ever seeing it.

The modern minivan has changed the way we do a lot of things. With the click of a button two doors slide open and multiple kids can jump in and out with the greatest of ease. There are more cup holders than seats and one automobile manufacturer put a vacuum cleaner inside the latest model of their minivan. Smart move.

There are lots of opinions out there about a DVD player inside the vehicle. While we don't use it every single time we leave the house, we have found that it is great for long trips and also stops the occasional screams and fights that come from the back seats.

Unless you mandate that the kiddos use headphones every time they watch a movie in the car, you will inevitably hear all the dialog, but will never see the movie because you are driving.

Recently I was sitting in the back with my kids and got a chance to actually see the video. I realized I knew every song and all the dialog, but I had a completely different idea in my head of what the characters looked like. I had never actually watched the movie. I have also considered taking the DVD out of the car and hiding in my office to finish watching the movie that had such gripping dialog.

Check out my viral video that describes this phenomenon.
bit.ly/FrozenDads (Note capital letters in link.)

Rule #88

You will get excited about cartoons again.

Remember when you were a kid and were super-excited about the latest cartoon? Some things will come full circle when you're an adult and this is one of them.

You know you are the parent of a preschooler (or even a schooler) when you get excited about a new Disney cartoon that is airing soon. You race to the remote to set the DVR and you mark the calendar so you don't forget about this exciting event.

This can also backfire on you. There have been many times that I have been watching a cartoon with my kids only to look around the room and realize that I am the only one in the room. I'm not sure when they left, but I am fully engrossed in what is happening on the screen and the kids are nowhere to be found.

BONUS RULE:

You will find yourself answering questions aloud that Mickey Mouse asks, singing along to theme songs, yelling at Mr. Noodle, and pondering how the letter K can afford to sponsor an entire TV show.

Rule #89
You will cheat without letting your children know.

When your four-year-old has to bring an empty cereal box to school for a project, it is possible, okay probable, that you won't have a cereal box in your cupboard that you are comfortable sending to school.

Case in point: I had to creatively explain to my oldest daughter why I needed to go buy one of those athlete-endorsed cereals, pour out the contents, and bring it to school in place of the chocolate-chip-cookie cereal box that we just emptied and was ready to go. Oh, stop criticizing me. I don't need that kind of judgment from you, too! Admit it, a bowl of cookies drenched in cold milk sounds delicious, especially after you've put your kids to bed and realize that you never actually ate dinner because you were not hungry at 5 p.m. when you fed everyone else.

Rule #90
Your children remember everything.

I could give any number of examples for this rule. I try to take each of my kids out once a week and have some special Daddy time, one-on-one. This gives you quality time with your kids and also scores you points with the spouse as they take some well-deserved time reading a funny parenting book, finishing the sit-com that has been paused for two weeks, or sleeping for a few more minutes.

Once when we were at our favorite pancake establishment for a Daddy-daughter date, and the waiter made the mistake of offering my daughter one of the syrups on the table. Upon hearing the options, one of them was completely out of the question. The word he said was boysenberry." The words my daughter heard were poison berry and she has refused to touch the stuff ever since. Thank you princess movies for ruining her opportunity to ever experience pancakes the way God intended.

Rule #91

You will have Scotch tape residue on the ceiling.

One of my kids' favorite activities is for me to tickle them. They like to be tickled until they can barely breathe. I hated that as a kid, but somehow they didn't get that gene and a regular after-dinner pastime involves me wrestling with them on the living room floor.

Needless to say, they have much more energy than I do, and it isn't long until I am lying supine on the floor, looking up and breathing heavy.

The other day, while in post-tickle repose, I noticed that my ceiling was speckled with invisible-tape residue. Surprisingly, my first thought was not to clean up this mess. It was actually sentimental, and I lay there reminiscing about why each piece of tape was there.

They were all remnants of past parties. The superhero party, the princess party, the dress-up fashion show, the cupcake party, the neighborhood haunted house. Each piece of tape had a story and I couldn't help but smile. They are all still stuck to my living room ceiling to this day.

BONUS RULE:

While lying on the floor I also noticed that little toy balls dropped on to the floor will roll under the sofa to the furthest corner and just out of reach.

Telling the Truth

Rule #92 **When your child starts forming full thoughts and sentences, their honesty will cause you to become extremely self-conscious.**

My perfect princess awoke early one morning and I bounded into her room to scoop her up, kiss her, and welcome her to the day when she sleepily squinted, frowned at me, and spoke her first words of the day, "Put a shirt on, Daddy. You look funny."

They will say other less-than-flattering and completely honest things to you such as: "Are those Mommy's shoes you are wearing?" "Mommy, you are too big to fit in here," and "Daddy, do you want to wear a bra?"

When my kid started talking, I joined a gym. True story.

Rule #93

When your kid runs into the room and announces, "I didn't poop!" it actually means, "I pooped!"

Children are notorious for telling the truth. There are numerous rules to support this. Sometimes there are exceptions to the rule when they realize a little lie might benefit them. A two year old's proclamation "I didn't poop!" is not intended to be a vicious lie, but simply the reaction of a child who doesn't want to stop playing to have her diaper changed. The moral of the story is, lies stink and Mommy and Daddy will always find out the truth.

Rule #94

Kids will make true (and funny) observations.

Small kids have an uncanny knack for saying the most truthful things. I saw my little princess sitting on the bottom stair step in our home. I could tell there was something that was troubling her and I knew the carefully chosen words of a father could turn this all around in an instant.

I sat down next to her on the step, peered into her sweet face and said, "Sweetheart, you have beautiful eyes." Without missing a beat she looked directly back at the man in her life, the hero that she thinks about most of the day, grabbed my face, and said, "Daddy...you have eyes, too."

Truthful and to the point.

Rule #95

Kids will call it like they see it.

I know you think telling the truth is a great quality, and it is. The problem is they have not yet been infused with a little thing called discernment in their repertoire. They will tell it like it is at the most inopportune moments, including things you and your spouse say about your neighbors or friends or family when you think no one is listening to you.

Often times, these little truth-tellers will say things to you or about you that are absolutely truthful, but will come at the wrong time.

One time when my wife had gone out for a well-deserved evening with her girlfriends; I was attempting to make dinner. It was a Murphy's Law kind of night where all of the kids were screaming, clamoring for my attention, wanting a toy, or demanding a certain episode of a cartoon. All the while the dinner was burning and the dishwasher was spitting out strange bubbles.

My two-year-old looked at me and simply said, "Daddy, you need help."

Rule #96

If you can't handle the truth, don't ask a toddler any question at all.

I have given many examples of how a child's little mind and mouth can work together to stop you in your tracks. You will stand in front of them at times with your mouth open, shaking your head slowly as you crack up over something they've said and done.

Mom had gone out for the evening and I took it upon myself to make dinner for the gang. As I mentioned before, I am notorious for making one thing at a time. Meals take eight times longer and things are always cold when the next course comes out.

Quite proud of myself for not burning the meal, I asked my daughter, "How is dinner tonight?"

I like to believe she pondered the least harmful, yet truthful answer as she said, "Well, it's not too yucky."

For Dads

Rule #97
Daddies of girls will know every Disney princess by name.

I recently indulged my daughter's determination to meet her favorite princesses and we made the trek down to Disneyland for the day. The line to meet the made-up actresses is rarely less than forty-five minutes long, and it always includes a winding array of fidgety young girls and their patient parents trying to keep them still until they finally get some face time with their heroines.

Despite the annoyingly long line that you wait in sometimes for hours, the look on your daughter's face and the hours of smiles that follow will be worth every single second in line and more. Priorities change.

I can also now add a bullet point to my resume that I could not have done a few years ago. As a Daddy of girls, I know every single princess by name. I know their clothes, their stories, their friends, their betrothed, and their nemeses. Go on, test me.

Rule #98

Shirtless dads will feel warm puke.

When babies are first born, mommies get all the instructions from the doctor and all the cards, flowers, and love, and rightfully so. I will gladly give up some spotlight time if I don't have to have to push a watermelon out of... anyway, I digress.

Mommies also get the mandate from the doctor to strip the baby down and do skin to skin contact with the baby. I understand this, and I am not knocking the positive effects of snuggle time for mom and baby, but dads rarely get this sort of directive.

One of my friend's pediatricians instructed the dad to take his shirt off while he holds the baby and do daddy skin-to-skin time. This was dubbed "Kangaroo Time" by the doctor. I had never heard that term before nor since. Now you know it, too.

Mommy gets to feed the baby and hand off the very full-of-milk kid to daddy for burping. Sometimes daddy will have his shirt off and is feeling the soft skin of his perfect child when all of a sudden a baby burp is immediately followed by a warm sensation running down his back.

Sure enough, the little booger has puked fresh, warm, delicious lunch all down dad's back, into his shorts, and onto the floor. This is immediately followed by dad handing the baby back to mom, mom laughing really hard, and dad getting on his knees to scrub the floor before jumping into the shower.

Rule #99
Men, you will walk around having adult conversations with a pink bow in your hair.

My daughters like to place their barrettes and bows in my hair and I let them do it. Yes, I'm also the same dad who constantly has remnants of sparkly pink nail polish on my toes and traces of glitter on my face, too. I figure they are only going to be this young once and I will one day miss the quality time playing with my little girls. After all, what do I have to lose? They are my princesses and we love to play together. My wife says it is very manly for me to be down on the floor playing with Barbies with my girls, and that's good enough for me.

One particular incident involved my exchange with a curious drive-thru employee whose eyes kept drifting upwards to the top of my head. Finally my self-awareness kicked in and I realized I indeed had a bright pink bow in my hair.

BONUS RULE:

As a Daddy to little girls I hope you will wear nail polish more often than not. I can't tell you the number of times I have gone out in public with purple toenails, hair bows and makeup. Not just because I live in Hollywood, but because my little princesses think that is just what you do. Playing is fun and important. Let them dress you up.

My daughter recently caught a glimpse of my clean, unpainted toenails and said, "Oh no, Daddy. Your nail polish came off."

Rule #100

Pregnancy brain never goes away (for fathers either).

"Pregnancy brain" affects millions of women each year and is a puzzling medical phenomenon. (See Rule #71.) My wife lost her wallet and/or keys four times in three weeks when she was hosting our last child in her uterus. Women have been known to put clothes on backwards, leave stoves on, and dry clothes in the dryer three times as a result of the sweet angel they are carrying who is quite certainly sucking up all of their brain cells. I'm here to attest to the fact that, unfortunately, it affects men too and does not quickly go away after the birth of your child.

Case in point: One day I was tasked with watching our three children. In the blink of an eye, I realized the youngest was missing. He was only thirteen months old, so he couldn't have gone far, but which way? Where should I start? I thought yelling his name would be a good way to begin, so I did that. I ran in one direction, then the other, and looked high and low. I did this for about fifteen seconds, which seemed like an eternity, before I found him. He was on my hip—I was holding him.

Pregnancy brain. It's a real thing. It'll get you too. Even if you are...uh... what was I saying?

Rule #101

With each child you add to the family, a percentage of your brain cells go away.

You will yell, "Stop it _____!" and say a child's name, another child's name, dog, cat, goldfish, and then scream. In that order.

If you have two children, you will call her the other kid's name first. If you have a dog and one child, you will call her the animal's name first.

This is part of the pregnancy brain phenomenon that even men suffer from. It's the reason you can't remember to lock the car, where you parked at the mall, or even why you went to the mall in the first place.

I believe the symptoms never truly go away. You are so occupied with a million different things as a parent it is sometimes difficult to focus. The last thing you want to do is take a second to think about whom among the brood you are actually speaking to.

So, be forewarned, when your toddler grabs the dog leash and heads for the open front door, you will yell everybody else's name just before you scoop her up in a panic as you finally remember the moniker you spent hours grueling over with your spouse.

For Moms

Never underestimate the healing power of a kiss.

Modern medicine and all of its advancements have allowed us to cure diseases, diagnose ailments on the internet (moms, lay off WebMD, you're just going to make yourself crazy), and revive people from near death, but nothing fixes a boo-boo like a single kiss from mom's sweet lips. I have seen hysterical, screeching, owie-ridden toddlers fall completely silent from this simple act.

I too have learned the sacred art of boo-boo kissing. One day my son held up a finger and said, "Dad, Dad, Dad, Dad, Dad, Dad, Dad, Dad..." I was distracted by something else that I'm sure was very important. On the 27th "Dad," I leaned toward his outreached finger only half glancing his way and said, "You have an owie?" as I gently kissed it. I immediately said, "That's not an owie is it?" and my son cheerfully replied, "It's snot!"

While a mother's tender form of first aid will heal almost anything during this brief time in their kids' lives, I must warn you, always look before you kiss.

Rule #103
Your palm, the back of your hand, and all ten digits automatically become perfectly calibrated scientific thermometers.

The calibration begins early in your child's life when you start sticking fingers into bottles and splashing milk on your wrist to make sure that the temperature is just right. This skill gradually perfects itself as you accurately determine temperature with a backhand to the forehead or a palm to a sick, sleeping kid's back.

Apparently the older you get, the more accurate your hand becomes. Elderly grandmothers can determine child temperatures down to one tenth of a degree. You have been given a gift. Go forth and become the master of touching foreheads to determine who gets to go to school and who doesn't!

Rule #104
There is no bag large enough when traveling with kids.

Despite your best efforts to "just pack a couple things" or "buy diapers when you get there," you will amass approximately six tons of necessary things for any overnight trip.

By the way, mommies are much better at this than daddies. Mommies remember to bring extra clothes for spit-ups, extra shoes, toys for the plane, movies for the car, and the little things like FOOD. Daddies usually see a ready-to-go diaper bag as one that has a diaper in it.

Rule #105

You will clench your teeth at offending statements.

We have already established that kids say whatever is on their minds. They will just tell the truth with both conviction and utter disregard for the feelings of anybody within earshot.

One afternoon with no prompting whatsoever, my honest angel was taking some time out to examine herself in the mirror. She blurted out the words that make any father with good sense run out of the room so as to not witness a crime: "Mommy, my butt is tiny but someday it will be big like yours."

Rule #106
You will say things you never thought would come out of your mouth.

"Get your toes out of that. I am trying to put eggs in there!"

This is just one example, but an absolutely real one. My toddler had been climbing up to the countertops since she could walk. We even rearranged living room furniture at one point to keep her from doing so, but she ended up moving chairs and couch cushions to build a climbable structure that she could scale to get to the food.

Finally, we gave up and just let her climb. She always wanted to help cook meals, but often times got sidetracked or bored and the above exclamation actually came from my wife's mouth during a breakfast preparation one morning.

Other things that I have been known to say include, "String cheese only goes in your mouth," and, "Don't keep bacon in your pillow case!"

Rule #107
Your kids will not have postpartum etiquette.

Having no real understanding of the finer points of the human anatomy, your children may say things that are less than edifying to you at any given moment. Such a moment came shortly after my wife gave birth to our third child. Needless to say, mommies' tummies are not immediately flat right after delivery.

A few days after her baby brother was home from the hospital, my very confused three-year-old looked at my wife's belly and said, "If Daddy's holding Asher, then who's in your tummy?"

Travel

Rule #108

You will empathize with the parents of the baby on the airplane that screams for forty minutes straight...because you've been there.

When you don't have kids, you may spend half the flight turning around, frowning, and shaking your head. When you do have kids you also make faces, but it is to make the little crier giggle in order to forget about the loud engine roar or his aching ears just for a minute.

You will also go out of your way to help that mother with her five carry-ons and her stroller as you deplane because once again, you've been there!

Rule #109

On cross country flights your children will poop twice as much as they do at home.

The scientific evidence is still under investigation, but for some reason your kids will crap themselves multiple times on airplanes. The mathematical formula looks something like this: If N is the number of diapers you have brought with you, your children's poops during the duration of your flight will be N+1.

This proven theorem is one thing, but it is twice as annoying when coupled with the fact that you are supposed to take your child into a bathroom that is smaller than a dollhouse closet and change him on a fold down table the size of a postage stamp.

Rule #110
You will learn to despise airport security screenings.

The Transportation Security Administration does a great job and serves a vital function, but if you travel with kids often, you will start to hate the ins and outs of airport security. Fold down the stroller and flip it upside down to put it on the belt. Take the car seat off the base and flip it over. Pull out the water for the formula and keep it separate—the list goes on.

I'm sure there are some things that are in a manual somewhere, but occasionally the spirit of the law is not considered when dealing with the airport security. When traveling with my children, I have been asked to remove their shoes multiple times. Yes, those tiny little baby shoes that don't have laces, tread, or leather. Even those little socks that are designed to look like shoes have had to occasionally go on the X-ray belt for screening.

Believe me, I am all for security and understand the necessity, but as a parent you simply want to scream out loud things like, "REALLY?" and, "OH, COME ON!" Trust me, don't say those things in the security line—it will only make things worse. Know that you are not alone, fellow parents. You and the seven or eight other people that read this book will be like-minded in knowing that we silently seethe together as we comply and remove baby socks for the "safety and security" of our homeland. Do I still seem bitter about this?

Rule #111
You will think about your children when they are not there.

I once was on a flight and briefly fell asleep. For some reason, I had a dream that my kid was about to spill a bowl of Cheerios. I woke up, lunged forward, and slammed my head into the back of the seat in front of me. True story.

Another time I was on a business trip and randomly smelled poop. I immediately missed my kids.

Rule #112
You will rearrange your entire life and schedule for your children.

It is not just cliché to say everything changes when babies come along. Your life, your meal times, bed times, and social calendar are forever altered when offspring are added into the mix.

Mommies and daddies will arrange travel schedules to take red-eyes or early morning flights to make it to dinner or to tuck in their kiddos.

You will find that spending time with them is invaluable. You'll leave work early to make a soccer game or recital. You will bend and rearrange the routine so you don't miss a moment of their childhood that is speeding by. You'll have the rest of your life to have a grown-up routine. This is the time to interrupt your schedule for them so you get to be present for the highs and the lows, the hugs and the skinned knees, and even the diapers. It's worth it.

Rule #113

Not every person sitting behind you on an airplane is playing peek-a-boo with your kid.

As a hard and fast rule, your child is absolutely the most adorable kid on the planet. He was knit perfectly together by God Almighty and is the most awesome human you've ever laid eyes on. Why others do not understand this will continually be beyond the scope of your understanding.

As proof that not all people see what you see, there will be times when you will be on an airplane (like I was recently) and assume the person behind you is playing with your precious angel.

I was holding my fourteen-month-old in my lap and the lady behind me was leaning forward. My princess kept giggling out loud at her, so in one quick movement I popped her over the top of the seat and exclaimed, "Peek-a-boo!" to the frowning businesswoman in 3B who was merely reaching forward to retrieve her laptop.

Now I looked like a crazy person that was playing human ventriloquist for a disinterested audience. Hopefully it made her smile later on as she sat in her important meeting thinking about the fool and his baby. But at the time, even a toothless, curly-red-haired cherub was not enough to break her concentration or offer a smile. Oh well, my kid retaliated with a soft, brown surprise that made everyone around us look at her. I'm sure that's all she wanted in the first place.

Rule #114

Children misunderstand the cutest words.

Following a family vacation, we returned to LAX airport and upon arrival at the gate, the flight attendant reminded us to gather our belongings. My five-year-old seriously asked, "Why would anyone pack bologna?"

Rows 4-7 thought that was hysterical, and my daughter learned for the first time that she was a natural comedienne.

Conversations and Quotes

Rule #115

Your kids will make unexpected proclamations.

In the middle of a crowded restaurant, my toddler decided to chime in and volunteer some information that was not necessary or welcome at that moment. She made no segue from the current conversation whatsoever.

Speaking to no one in particular, she loudly made the announcement, "It hurts when I poop!"

Rule #116

Your children will have deeply profound statements that make you wonder if they are more intellectual than you are.

Example:
Me: Don't be ridiculous, Lilah.
Lilah: I'm not ridiculous. I'm a girl!

At this I wondered if she had been talking to her mother, had an audience with Gloria Steinem, or was trying to teach me something. At any rate, I left it alone and simply said, "You are absolutely right."

Rule #117
You will dread certain sentences.

You will stop what you are doing, close your eyes, exhale, and shake your head when you hear these words shouted from the other room: "Daddy, come clean this up!"

It really could be anything, and your mind will race trying to guess what in the world it is this time. No matter how good of a guesser you think you are, you will always be surprised. Speaking from experience, I have seen everything from puzzle pieces to an exploded jar of spaghetti sauce.

Rule #118
The things you say will not come out the way you intended.

Brothers and sisters will always fight. They will brawl over balloons, hair bows, toy trucks, or who Daddy loves best. This is just a natural phenomenon that has and always will exist.

Recently we had a few bad days of yelling, hitting, and screaming. For some reason I had to leave the room for a moment. I actually spouted this nonsense before I left: "I will be back in a few minutes. Do not hurt each other until I get back!"

Rule #119
Your sense of humor is contagious and will rub off on your children.

Whether you like it or not, your children will act like you. This statement alone should force most of us to take a deep breath. The things that come out of your children's mouths are like little recordings that remind you of precisely the things you say and the way you say them.

Once my daughter was in the corner making the straining face that only a toddler makes when there is a surprise brewing in the diaper.

I asked, "Are you pooping, sweetie?" With a grimace and a grunt she replied, "Yes, and I'm making it extra stinky just for you."

Okay. Hopefully that is something that I have never said, but the humor and intention behind the statement sounded just like me. She said it for the specific purpose of making me laugh—and she succeeded.

Rule #120
You will make ridiculous threats and they won't question it.

I have said this next statement on more than one occasion, and I don't even mean to say it. When getting ready for school I was so frustrated that they were not in the car on time I actually said, "This car is going to go to school with or without you!"

Now obviously that made no sense whatsoever, as I would probably need good cause to drive to an elementary school at 7:45 in the morning with no children on board. For some reason the very notion terrified my little munchkins and it sent them scrambling. I think by eighth grade they might catch on, but in the meantime, let's keep it our little secret.

Rule #121
Kids speak from their point of view.

Children have wonderful imaginations and brilliant minds that absorb everything around them at an alarming rate. Also, they only have a perception of their own reality. In the strictest sincerity they will say things that will make you shake your head and say, "Thaaaanks."

My daughter once said, "My kitty cat is really old, Daddy. Kind of like you."

Rule #122 Children will demand that you become a magician.

If there is a favorite toy, food, or sippy cup that you have forgotten at home, your toddler will demand that you produce the object on the spot.

This usually happens in a vehicle when there is no possible way you can get to the baby doll with the purple dress. The conversation, which has absolutely no basis in logic, usually goes like this:

Kid: I want my baby doll.
Parent: We left it at home.
Kid: But I want it.
Parent: Sorry, we left it at home.
Kid: But I need it.
Parent: I already told you we do not have it with us. It is physically not here.
Kid: (Volume rising) BUT I WANT IT!
Parent: (Matching the volume) WE DON'T HAVE IT!!

This is usually followed by the kid crying and the parent wanting to cry.

Rule #123
You will smile and laugh nervously when out in public.

Because they are autonomous little beings, you can never predict exactly what kids are going to say—especially in a crowded shopping mall. My daughter saw a lady walking toward us and pointed directly at her shouting, "You look like grandma!"

A million things flashed through my head as I wanted to say, "Her grandma is young and pretty," or "You are not that old," or countless other things that didn't seem appropriate.

When this happens to you, one option is to keep walking and pretend like you don't know the kid. Another option is to laugh out loud, roll your eyes, and say, "Oh silly girl." Then grab her hand and run for the exit. You could also just walk over to the lady and say, "Can I drop them off on Tuesday while my wife and I go out to dinner?"

Thankfully, the lady had a sense of humor and was most likely a grandmother herself so she just smiled and said, "Why, thank you." It could've been worse.

Rule #124

Your kids won't give you a second to think.

While talking to my two-year-old daughter about something she had asked me, I briefly paused mid-sentence to think of exactly how I was going to phrase the next thought so she could understand what I was saying. Letting no time pass, she interrupted my thought by saying, "If you can't remember things, I will just write them down for you."

Rule #125

Your kids become very serious about art projects. Try not to laugh.

This can best be summarized with this verbatim dialog I had with my three year old.

Lilah: Daddy, look at my Play-Doh project.
Me: It's beautiful.
Lilah: Do you like it?
Me: I sure do, sweetheart. What is it?
Lilah: I call it the orange turd!

Rule #126

Priorities will change altogether.

This falls into the category of the, "I knew that rule. Now tell me something I don't know," but there are lots of ways priorities change and you will be better for it.

I pride myself on being a football fan. I love the NFL. I have a favorite team. I try to catch all the games and a losing Sunday actually puts me in a funk for a few hours.

When you have children, everything changes. I don't watch games nearly as often as I did before kids. Most of the time updates on my phone are the best I can do, and sometimes even then I have to wait until the Sunday night wrap-up to know the final score.

One Sunday my daughter was preoccupied in another room and I thought it would be a great opportunity to switch on the game and get a quick update. No sooner than the high definition logos flashed across the screen, my three-year-old ran back into the room and innocently asked aloud, "Why is there football on my Snow White television?"

Good question.

With my priorities now properly in check, I promptly switched the TV back to what it was obviously intended for as she snuggled up next to me.

Rule #127

Lunches will often be hysterically funny.

My wife was away on a photo shoot one afternoon and I was tasked with making lunches for everyone. Unlike my wife, who has learned that it is impossible to please all of the food requests and now just makes one like-it-or-lump-it meal, I tried to make what each kid wanted.

When I got around to the five-year-old, I asked her what she would like for lunch. After sincerely pondering this for about seven seconds, she responded, "Chicken." "Great," I said. "What kind of chicken would you like?" Her serious response was probably the greatest in culinary history when she said, "Just a dead one."

Trying not to laugh, I asked what kind of dead one. She took me by the hand, walked to the fridge, opened it, pointed, and said, "That dead one." Sure enough, there on the shelf of our refrigerator was a dead chicken. My wife had gone to the supermarket and bought a whole roasted chicken the night before.

I carved up some dead chicken. She ate two plates.

Rule #128

Never underestimate the wisdom of a child.

"Dad, I have a problem," stated my five-year-old.

Sensing this was about something fairly important—at least important to a five-year old—I got down on her level to assess the situation. "What's the problem?" I inquired.

"The things that are the yummiest to eat are not that healthy."

And there you have it. A profound statement from someone who is less than 2,000 days old.

Rule #129

When trying to get your kids to eat, be mindful of how you phrase things.

When trying to be a decent parent you start thinking about things that you have never consciously thought about before—such as keeping another human being alive. It is now solely up to you, and maybe your spouse, to provide healthy food for your progenies.

One of the strange things that starts to happen over and over again is that you become like your own parents. You say the actual words that your parents said to you such as, "Eat your vegetables and fruits."

In an attempt to do just that, I wanted my kids to enjoy some dried apricots that we had just purchased. Thinking they would naturally love them like their daddy does, I handed them each a slice and watched as their curious minds looked at the texture and contemplated putting the squishy, odd-shaped thing in their mouths.

They were all ready to give it a shot when yours truly made the ultimate mistake and said the first thing that came to mind which was, "You will love it. It's just like eating a big, juicy ear!"

That was it. Not doing it. The "ears" were promptly passed back to me and I'm fairly sure I have ruined dried apricots for them for life.

Rule #130

Remember their limited knowledge of our vernacular and proceed accordingly.

I live in Southern California. One of the blessings and curses about our climate is that it rarely gets really cold. My kids never see snow unless it is during the holidays when one of the local malls pumps that awesome faux snow into the air. It looks exactly like snow even when it is eighty degrees outside. I realize this is not a thing in most parts of the country, but it makes sense that my kids would not be privy to certain expressions.

My wife used a phrase that was lost on the three-year-old. She said it was "bitter cold outside." My daughter freaked out. After discussing this with her, we discovered it was because she assumed the air could literally bite her and she really did not want to be chomped by an unseen force if she dared going out the door. It took about ten minutes of parent-child counseling, but we finally convinced her that the air does not actually have teeth.

BONUS RULE:

Unfortunately because it rains so little in Los Angeles, my little boy confused the words rain and snow. It was quite cute when he asked if he could play in the snow and grabbed his superhero umbrella. Boys love puddles. It's worth it to invest in a pair of rubber boots and a superhero umbrella for your little man to go outside and splash with fervor. Once again, depending on your geography, this may be daily or twice a year. Until he was two-years-old, my son was terrified of the wet stuff falling from the sky. I have videos for blackmail... er...to prove it.

Rule #131

Be prepared for lots of backhanded compliments.

If you have learned anything from this book so far it should be that kids are brutally honest and will say exactly what is on their minds. In fact, it is a great litmus test for what is actually going on in your life, home, habits, actions, words, and looks. They will see it, assess it, and say it.

There was the time when I probably had not bathed in a day or so for one reason or another, and my daughter noticed. Parents, get used to it. Especially stay-at-home parents. You may as well just mark Thursdays on the calendar to try and get a shower in.

I had taken a shower and scooped my three-year-old daughter up shortly after when she honestly offered me this compliment: "Daddy, now you smell different."

Rule #132

Kids are natural negotiators and will attempt to bargain with you.

I don't remember how this started, but my wife and I got into a negotiating phase with our kids that would take a highly paid contract lawyer to sort out.

The children would try to strike up deals about everything from Disneyland trips to post-dinner ice cream. At first it was cute; then we realized we were either breeding politicians or lobbyists. The deal-making was getting more outrageous.

During a grueling bath-time battle my daughter offered this compromise, "I will take a bath if you promise I will not get wet." I'm no lawyer, but I'm sure that kind of bargaining doesn't leave me with a lot of options for compromise.

BONUS RULE:

"Because I said so" still trumps everything. Regardless of the bargaining power of the little litigators in training, you still have full authority and veto power over, well, everything. When the negotiations get too overwhelming or in my case, when you know you've been outsmarted, just say that statement and it stops the deal making—because I said so.

Rule #133

Your children will almost grasp big people concepts.

My kids love art. They have an art table where they spend a good portion of the day coloring, painting, and cutting out pieces of paper to glue onto other pieces of paper. It's just what our kids do.

Recently my four-year-old graduated from the "Dad, can you cut this for me" phase to safety scissors that she uses in preschool. It was a welcome promotion as it gained me about ten minutes every day so I could do something besides cut out dolls and other accessories.

Somewhere along the way, my daughter must have heard the age-old adage about what not to do with scissors because she came up to me with a sincere face (and voice to match) and said, "Daddy, when I get big can I run with scissors?" I laughed out loud and proceeded to explain why it was not a great idea for any of us to do such a thing. Despite the silliness of it all, I do admire her inquisitive nature and her willingness to want to do big people things.

Rule #134
You will say just plain ridiculous things.

It is not exactly sage wisdom I just extolled in this rule, and we have been over this a bit already. Much like the time I made those invisible cookies for my children, my wife also went temporarily insane and the proof came out of her mouth.

Our oldest two girls are less than two years apart. Because they are so close in age, they are each other's best friend and worst enemy. They play together beautifully and will not fall asleep unless they are two feet apart. That said, they are equally deviant to one another when they are angry.

I remember one incident that involved fighting over who was going to be She-Ra. Yes, you read that correctly. They had watched that fantastic 1980s cartoon that my wife got them hooked on, and were going through a phase of only wanting to play She-Ra: a warrior princess. Most of the time everything worked out well and they played without much debate over casting issues.

One day, however, the climate was different and tempers flared. As they screamed at each other over who was actually going to play the title character in the upcoming play session, I walked in just in time to hear my wife intervene with the following command: "You are BANNED from using your imagination!! No one gets to be She-Ra, and you can't pretend ANYTHING until I say so!"

Rule #135

Your kids will correct ~~how you say stuff~~ **your grammar.**

Your children desperately want to be grown-ups. They will emulate your every move. It is eye-opening as well as frightening when your little one starts to act like you. It's like having a little mirror follow you around all day showing you the best and worst sides of yourself.

My two-year-old has taken to correcting me on occasion. It is cute, and it shows me that she is actually listening to what is going on around her (which I hope is a positive thing).

The other day I asked her if she was ready for her lunch and she replied, "Daddy, it's not SAMwich. It's SANDwich. Ask me if I want a peanut butter and jelly SANDwich." This coming from the kid who was wearing a "bwack and wed dwess"! Sheesh.

Rule #136 — The amazing logic of children will crack you up.

A typical conversation between my two-year-old and me:

Haley: What is this?
Me: It's a to-go snack we eat in the car. Where are you going?
Haley: To the garage to sit in the car so I can eat it.

Rule #137 — Children hear exactly what you say.

Until they understand sarcasm, your offspring will take to heart the literal words that come out of your mouth. Sarcasm is, in my opinion, a form of humor that you must use just to survive some of the insanity of raising children. Be careful what you say and how you say it.

There are a lot of examples I could offer to make my point, but here is a recent one: on a trip to Disneyland, my kids were falling asleep in the car. Knowing that the drive time to Anaheim was going to align with my two-year-old's nap schedule, I made a simple statement. "Sweetheart, just close your eyes for a bit and when you open them we will be there."

My brilliant toddler, missing the hyperbole, did exactly what I told her to do. She shut her eyes as tightly as she could for about three seconds and opened them wide expecting to see Mickey welcoming her. It didn't happen. She was upset. Somehow that was my fault.

Rule #138
Kids can be so sweet that you will wish you didn't have to puke.

I was extremely sick with a stomach virus. It had made the rounds through our household and I was the last to get it. I was quarantined to a guest bedroom on a different floor of the house and rarely saw anyone else, unless it was during my sprints to and from the bathroom.

While I was in the guest bed, lying in a sweaty mess and praying for death or relief, whichever was quicker, I heard a faint tapping as my three-year-old barely knocked on the door.

I raised my feeble head and beckoned her to come in when she quietly whispered, "Daddy, what color is your mouth?"

"I...uh...it's...who wants to know?" I responded.

"I do," she said. "I am drawing a picture of you to make you feel better and I need to remember what color your mouth is."

Yep, that's a heart-melter. Nothing will make you get well quicker than your sweet kid working on an art project to make you feel better.

Rule #139 Children will offer outrageous observations.

Your children have the innate ability to say the greatest things ever. Their innocent minds and matching vocabularies can strike a chord that will make your heart smile. At times they can be so sweet. And at other times....

Case in point: After I had offered some nugget of brilliant comedy to my kids and they burst out laughing at whatever hilarity I had just created, my three-year-old regained her composure long enough to say, "You are one of the funniest daddies I have ever had."

Another observation came when I was shaving my face. My four-year-old walked in and said, "Daddy, the hair on top of your head goes inside and pops out on your face, right?"

Rule #140

Your kids will be brutally honest (and by that I mean brutal).

I heard the screams and cries from the two year old in the back yard. I raced out to see what was going on. I was greeted by the four-year-old who said, "Haley is crying."

"I can see that," I said. "Did you say something to hurt her feelings?"

"No. I didn't Daddy. I wouldn't do that. She's probably crying because I pushed her off the slide."

Rule #141

Parents must always be prepared for honest feedback from their children.

I could write an entire book of entries that would fit under this heading. One of the many awesome things about your children is their honesty. Until about age four or five they have not perfected the art of manipulation, so they will just say whatever is on their little minds.

Once I was shaving in my bathroom and my sweet three-year-old came in and asked why I was putting foam on my face. I explained that it helps daddies get the hair off of their faces. Her well-meaning mind started to churn and she said: "Maybe you should think about rubbing it on your tummy, too"

BONUS RULE:

Kids will be straightforward at the wrong time. When the waitress asked if we needed anything else, my three-year-old announced, "My butt hurts."

Rule #142
During the most inopportune moment your child will say whatever comes to mind.

Sometimes their observation will come at just the right moment when it can best embarrass you. There are a number of examples I could give to support my evidence for this but I will simply describe one situation.

We were in Malibu for the dedication of a local park. There were a lot of people and speeches and noise. My daughter could have picked any one of the noisy moments to reveal what was on her mind. Instead she chose the exact (and only) moment in the day when there was complete and total silence, absolute dead air, record-scratch-style tranquility. The moment right after the entire crowd finished singing our National Anthem, into the reverent silence she shouted, "Daddy. Daddy! This booger looks like an artichoke!"

Being the good father that I am, what do you think I did?

1. Look the other way as if to say, "Who is the mortified man this child is speaking to?"
2. Shush her and tell her to not speak so loud?
3. Scoop her up and whisk her away from frowning adults?

Nope. Remember, I'm her dad. I promptly bent down to look at it, then stood back up to hundreds of eyes staring at me and said aloud to no one and everyone, "At least she knows her vegetables."

Rule #143 Confidence is a good thing.

I told my two-year-old son he had a cool light saber toothbrush and he said, "Yes! Cool like me." The same night I told my four-year-old that she was a very good reader. She said, "And a good thinker, too!"

Rule #144 The similes kids come up with are fascinating.

Kids have amazing and imaginative minds. They are creative and quick. Sometimes you will have no idea where they come up with the things they say. Take it all in. This is the greatest time in your life. Then they get older and it is the new greatest time in your life, too.

My four-year-old said, "Dad, I have to go pee as bad as the sun is hot."

I'm not exactly sure science can provide us with an exact correlation to this statement, but I'm pretty sure she really needed to go. Before she melts into a puddle, let's get her to the bathroom in a hot second. See what I did there? [Rim Shot]

Rule #145

The kitchen is a great place for learning.

They will learn about science and time and ingredients and all kinds of great life lessons here in the kitchen. Decades of great conversations with our kids will happen in the kitchen. Memories are made here. As I shared earlier, throughout childhood my wife found the kitchen to be a place of connection, creativity, and provision for her family, and that continues to this day. She is an incredible cook and baker and she is teaching our kids the basics of cooking even when they can't reach the counter.

The kitchen is definitely a gathering place in our home and where many of the sayings in this book have been recorded. The following story is no exception.

While having some kitchen fun with my wife, my three-year-old was seated at the center kitchen island filling us in on just how smart she was, as well as stating some of her limitations. She exclaimed, "I know where eggs, milk, and cheese come from, but what about elephants?"

Great question, where do elephants come from? Just as long as she doesn't ask about babies for a few more years, we're good. We can talk about elephants, and for now the answer is "Africa and Asia."

Rule #146
Kids will fight over the pronunciation, existence, and meaning of words.

One minivan fight on the way to school was over whether or not the word was hurricane or hurricake.

I was determined not to intervene. Besides, I was laughing too hard to be of much help anyway. Finally one of them asked me to settle the dispute. I responded correctly (I think), but it didn't help. The strong-willed princess was determined that the word was actually hurricake. I think I like that answer better anyway.

I also recently got into a very heated argument with my two-year-old son over whether or not the prehistoric animal was called a "dinosword".

Rule #147

"Sminit" is a word to a five-year-old.

The translation of that word is "Thank you, father, for repeatedly encouraging me to get in the car. I will simply be one more minute. Thanks for your patience."

We have more arguments over this one word than just about anything else. On average it takes about fifteen minutes per child to actually get into the vehicle and go somewhere. If you have four children, you must start one hour prior to the time you plan to pull your car out of the driveway.

Much of the time "sminit" is used by your offspring as they finish coloring, eating a sandwich, watching the last part of a cartoon, or finding their shoe.

Rule #148

Your children's prayers can wander just like ours.

Have you ever earnestly tried to pray and something just...happens? Your mind wanders or you start thinking and accidentally praying about things that you didn't mean to. You know you've done it. You are tired, it's late, and you lie in bed starting to thank the Almighty or ask His special favor over something... all of a sudden you are talking to Him about characters on a TV show that are not even real.

I think we all do that. Even kids. Their prayers can ramble as they browse the room. Prayer time with my four-year-old once went like this: "Dear God, thank you for my family, and my sister, and my brother, and food, and toys, and light bulbs, and tee shirts, and princesses. Amen."

Rule #149 Your children will read the signs.

My five-year-old really wanted to learn to read before going to kindergarten. She practiced sounding words out phonetically all the time. Unfortunately, there was a "Happy Hour" sign showing the specials at the pool's bar while we were on vacation. In a loud voice she proudly yelled, "Look Daddy, the happy whore starts at 5 p.m."

Rule #150 You will survive.

While you are in the midst of parenting craziness there are many times that you will question, "Does it get better?" "Am I a horrible parent?" "What am I saying?!" Don't doubt yourself, fellow soldier. We are all on this amazing, insane journey of parenting together. It does get better and it's all worth it.

Train them up in the ways they should go and when they are old they will not depart from it. You will survive! In the meantime, rely on this book and fellow parents to keep you sane.

Absolutely Real Conversations that Took Place in My Household

Me: You want a cheeseburger?
Asher (age 2): (Jams finger in nose) These boogers?
Me: No. Cheeseburger.
Asher: No thanks.

Lilah: I'm hungry.
Me: We'll get something the second we get home.
Lilah: No! I want something the FIRST we get home.

Me (to 2-yr-old son): People say you and I look the same.
Asher: I'm sorry.

Lilah: I can't really pick my nose today.
Me: Why?
Lilah: I have a hurt finger.

Haley: Do all houses have chimneys?
Lilah: Not the ones that celebrate Hanukkah.

Lilah: I don't like mini-cupcakes.
Me: You've had five.
Lilah: It took me a while to decide.

Haley: Daddy, I have a question.
Me: Yes, sweetheart.
Haley: Do you think princesses toot? Because I don't think Aurora does.

Lilah: Haley, when you get to Kindergarten you will learn to spell. Let's practice. What is S-L-E-E-P?
Haley: Apple.
Lilah: No. It spells sleep.
Haley: You didn't let me finish! I was going to say Apple is not what it spells!

Absolutely Real Quotes that
Were Said in My Household

I imagine if I could feel my poop it would feel like Play-Doh.
-Lilah, age 4

When you grow up, you get married so you will have someone to talk to. Otherwise it would be boring.
-Lilah, age 4

There is a certain doll I'm looking for. Peel your eyes out for it.
-Lilah, age 4

Sometimes when we cry and whine, it makes Mommy's neck hurt.
-Lilah, age 5

Dad, pretend like you're the evilest bad guy in the world, and your name is Rainbow Flower Girl.
-Haley, age 4

Dad! Come in here. My butt door won't open wide enough. I need help squeezing this poop out.
-Lilah, age 4

Um...I don't want to tell you this, but my ear just tooted.
-Lilah, age 5 during airplane descent

Daddy, I'm trying to go to sleep but I close my eyes and my mouth keeps talking.
-Lilah, age 6

I want to draw a butt and I'm trying to see what one looks like.
-Lilah, age 4 while going around in circles with her pants around her ankles

My friend Brooke's mom has twin babies. It's okay though because moms have two boobies.
-Lilah, Age 4

I'm not sucking on a pacifier, I'm just holding it in my mouth for my little brother.
-Haley, age 4

Daddy, brother's belly button fell off. Now he's a real boy!
-Haley, age 2

I'm not stealing the toy. I'm making her share.
-Haley, age 3

Can't we play what I want to for a change?! I'll even give you all my powers.
-Lilah, age 6

Let's pretend to be kids who are actually sisters that are pretending to be friends.
-Lilah, age 5

For the rest of my life I will know which shoe to put on my right foot because of this Band-Aid.
-Haley, age 4

This book is exactly like the one we have at home, just different pages and different words!
-Haley, age 4

You can't just be a mermaid when you grow up, you have to be born one.
-Lilah, age 5

Dear Lord, thank you for volcanoes, rainbows, people, and stores. Amen.
-Haley, age 4

God, thank you for Mommy, Daddy, Lilah, and Haley. In Jesus' name, oatmeal.
-Asher, age 2

Glossary of Things You Need To Know as a Parent

adding a -y sound at the end of a word: A communication device employed by parents so children will understand the noun you are trying to say. Examples: blanky, sippy, paci, wubby.

baby germs: The extremely powerful bacteria that will be sneezed directly into your open mouth at some point.

blowout: A bad word. When the poop crosses over the elastic barrier in the diaper effectively staining a onesie, cute dress, clothes, etc. Usually mom or dad also gets soiled in the process.

jj78eyj34yy7yjhkmn,h: Outgoing text messages from your cell phone during the baby and toddler phase.

kangaroo time: Skin-to-skin time for daddy and baby. Warning: men should not tell other dude friends about this. It will be an endless source of ribbing from their buddies from now on.

latch: Vitally important term that mommies will use a lot. Has nothing to do with a door, window, or drawer.

meconium: Sticky black stool in the first few days after a baby birth. Made of epithelial cells, amniotic fluid, and other big words. The main thing to remember is this is weird in color and so sticky.

Mexican: Best all-around family restaurant due to the quick chips and salsa that hits the table moments after you sit down.

minivan: A vehicle you once thought was "uncool" but now has become a luxurious ride that only the parents of 3+ kids can truly appreciate.

nipple: Not what it used to mean. Other words will usually accompany this noun including "flow," "cleanliness," and "pump."

parent vernacular: A series of nonsensical words parents use regularly that made no sense before having children. Examples: Pottette, Bumbo, Boppy, Moses Basket, Hooter Hider, Peepee Teepee, Wubanub, exersaucer, Soothies, Ergo Baby, Baby Bjorn, gripe water, Pack 'n' Play, Diaper Genie, bassinet, Jumperoo, double jogger, Mobi Wrap

sarcasm: A form or humor that you must use just to survive some of the insanity of raising children.

seepage: Similar to a blowout, but not as bad. Usually involves liquid.

sippy cup: A container with a spill-proof lid that children use for drinking. These will often be filled with three-day-old milk and are usually found under the sofa.

sminit: The word a five-year-old says when they need an extra minute or ten to do anything you ask them to do.

tinkle spigot: The device that controls the flow of liquid from a large container (such as a bladder). A word Ryan made up just for this book in Rule #18.

Stage 3 or "Crap Fest": The last phase of a poop threat level that sends a parent running to change a diaper as quickly as possible.

swaddling: The art of making a baby burrito. You will get angry at how quick the nurses do this in the hospital. You will practice at home and within a week, you will master the technique.

Uncrustables: One of the tastiest substances on the planet.

Tough Questions You Will Have To Answer

Why do my shoes have tongues?

Who's my baby doll's daddy?

What kind of farm did the dog go live on?

Why is there a moon out in the daytime?

Why does a lamb's tail shake three times and how long is that?

Why would anyone call this thing a tomato?

Where does lightning come from?

Why do my eyes water when I cry?